INVEST IN LIVING

101 WILD PLANTS FOR THE KITCHEN

The *Invest in Living* Series

INVEST IN LIVING

101 WILD PLANTS FOR THE KITCHEN

by

Geoffrey Eley

EP Publishing Limited
1977

71G

Acknowledgments

I have already declared my debt, in my companion book—*Wild Fruits and Nuts*—to all those authors, from the Rev. Gilbert White onwards, whose works I have collected since boyhood. In addition to my long experience of using Nature's own free larder, I wish to acknowledge the help I have been given in preparing this second volume by the immense knowledge of writers such as the historian Dorothy Hartley, whose classic *Food in England* (1954) is unsurpassed; and, coming more up to date, Richard Mabey whose *Food for Free* (1972) has proved invaluable as a check-list in making doubly sure that no plants are included in my book of which there can be any doubt as to their wholesomeness.

About the author

Dr Geoffrey Eley lives in the deep countryside he writes about—in a Victorian cottage in the Vale of Belvoir.

He was for some years producer of BBC farm and garden programmes as well as himself being a broadcaster. He has edited specialist journals concerned with agricultural science and medicine; in 1962 he launched *Medical News* as Britain's first weekly newspaper for doctors. Geoffrey Eley MA is a Fellow of the Royal Society of Medicine and a Member of the Royal Society of Literature.

Copyright © EP Publishing Ltd 1977

ISBN 0 7158 0489 8

Published 1977 by EP Publishing Ltd, East Ardsley, Wakefield, West Yorkshire WF3 2JN

Filmset in 'Monophoto' Univers 10 on 11 pt by
Richard Clay (The Chaucer Press) Ltd, Bungay, Suffolk
and printed in Great Britain by
G. Beard & Son Ltd, Brighton

Contents

Introduction

It is odd, but almost certainly true, that a country woman in the Middle Ages knew more about wild plants and their culinary and medicinal uses than does a housewife of today.

The reason is twofold: in the first place, the medieval family living frugally in the countryside needed to seek out and use as much wild food as they could—fruits, nuts, plants and roots as well as meat and fish. Then, a large degree of self-sufficiency, and therefore knowledge, was essential; in today's society, with mass-produced food available to all over the shop counter, neither a knowledge of nature's larder nor the economic motive are necessary for survival. The second reason for our comparative ignorance is that with modern medical techniques and drug therapy we no longer need to identify and use plants for medicinal purposes or 'magic' properties (albeit plants are still the source of many medicinal preparations). Even most of the herbs the town family uses in the kitchen now come from the factory, not the hedgerow or garden.

But changes are taking place. With greater leisure time more families are not merely driving into the countryside but are actively making better use of that free time by studying the ecology of different areas, learning something of their geology and archaeology, of country crafts and agriculture, of wild life and plant life. Documentary and entertainment programmes on television, the growth of countryside camping and walking, school studies and lavish natural history books—all these reflect a renewed and practical interest in our countryside heritage.

In this book my aim is to help readers to know when, where and what to harvest what is good to eat and how best to enjoy it. To this extent my book is neither entirely botanical, nor is it yet another 'cook book'. It is a guide to the correct ways of identifying and using wild plants as free food.

And, I hope, the book is easy to learn from, adequately illustrated as it is with accurate line drawings to assist the 'self-help' beginner. Not only are all the edible species listed on a season-by-season basis, so that you search for a particular food at exactly the right time of year, but the plants are grouped alphabetically within sections dealing with Leaves for Cooking, Leaves for Salads, Roots Worth Eating, Stems for Cooking, Useful Wild Herbs and, finally, Seaweeds to Enjoy.

This layout of the text makes this practical handbook quite different from any other published work on wild plants. I began, however, by referring to the greater knowledge of food plants which country folk had as a matter of course in bygone days, and some acknowledgment must therefore be made of the debt I and many other writers owe to early literature on the properties and identification of plants. At its simplest, we now know from the practical experiments of the early observers those plants to leave strictly alone because they kill or make us ill; but we also know—even though most of us today have to be informed afresh—plants whose leaves, stems or roots are useful human food.

The knowledge has been passed on by the writings of botanists and nature lovers, largely starting with the sixteenth-century herbals which first identified and described plants by way of text and beautiful drawings. This, too, was the time when magic gave way to a study of the genuine medicinal properties of many plants and the writing of more scientific books. By the nineteenth century, and with developing printing techniques, came a large number of natural history books revealing the secrets of the countryside to the ordinary townsman reader as distinct from the botanical and medical academics—a publishing vogue which has gone on ever since. As given briefly and in simple language in this book, some knowledge of the historical associations and early myths surrounding our familiar plants undoubtedly adds to one's interest in finding and using food plants—areas to which current books by Geoffrey Grigson, Dorothy Hartley, Michael Allaby, Richard Mabey and others have made such a distinguished contribution for reference and further study such as I have enjoyed.

All edible plants are best picked young, so I have grouped the species into the months when they first come into flower, thus indicating the best time to pick the leaves as food. To make it still easier, references are given alphabetically (not, be it said, in order of usefulness!) and—as with my *Wild Fruits and Nuts*—the book includes as many cookery hints and ways of enjoying edible plants as I have been able to collect from half a century of 'rural rides', during which I have visited at least once every county in the British Isles.

For readers who do not have *Wild Fruits and Nuts*, my companion volume in this series, it is necessary to repeat a bit of advice for those seeking food plants:

1. Make sure you identify your plants correctly from the descriptions and illustrations given in this book; you will also find that the *way* you cook or eat wild plants is important (also see poisonous plants list).

2. Avoid picking wild food from busy road verges where weed-killers and traffic fumes might contaminate plants; or where dogs are exercised regularly.

3. Do not become a plant vandal. Think of the survival of plant life for future generations and pick only in reasonable quantities. Remember that it is a legal offence to uproot some plants.

4. Have regard for private property, farm crops and at all times observe the country code by, for instance, shutting gates, avoiding hedgerow damage, being careful about fire risk and being sure not to spoil the countryside with litter.

1. Leaves for Cooking

January—March

In early spring, just at the time we need most green food for vitamins, it is scarcest and often expensive. Winter greens are over and spring greens not yet fit to eat—yet no house need be without a dish of greenstuff.

Chickweed

This low-growing plant is found everywhere throughout the British Isles. Its Latin name, *Stellaria media* indicates star-like flowers, and it blooms in even the severest winter weather, when the seeds provide food for small birds.

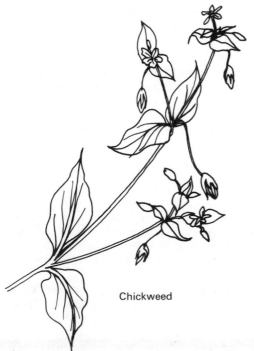

Chickweed

Water chickweed, *Myosoton aquaticum*, can be found straggling on river banks or in patches at the edge of damp woods, but it is rare in Wales and Scotland. It differs from common chickweed by having leaves which are bigger, fleshy and hairless.

To eat: Use chickweed leaves as a green vegetable, cooking them in a little boiling water. Or they can be eaten fresh in a salad.

Local names: chicken's meat, East Anglia; cluckenwort, Northumberland; mischievous Jack, Somerset; and murren, in Yorkshire.

Cleavers

Alternative, descriptive names for this very common plant of the hedgerow are sticky billy, hug-me-close and goosegrass. The stem, leaves and small round fruits have hooked hairs which catch on the clothing of passers-by. The name goosegrass comes from the fact that it was formerly fed to goslings.

This plant (Latin name *Galium aparine*) is very useful because it can be picked in winter, particularly in frosty weather when there is little else about; pick it before the hard round seeds appear, and boil it as a spinach.

Local names: Even if goosegrass is not among the better edible wild plants we seek today, it has a very long list of the most intriguing local names—including beggar weed in Nottinghamshire; blood-tongue, in Northumberland and Scotland (Gerard said, 'being drawne along the toong it fetcheth bloud'); clinging sweethearts, Wiltshire; cling rascal and clitche buttons, Devon; doctor's love, Somerset; gentlemen's tormenters, Suffolk;

Cleavers

huggy-me-close, Dorset; lizzie-run-the-hedge, Northumberland; and, remembering the plant's medical use, in Yorkshire and Cheshire goosegrass is called scurvy-grass.

Coltsfoot

A harbinger of spring this one, its bright yellow flower heads on pink-scaled stems coming in February before the leaves. It is a favourite with children who pick it everywhere on waste land, roadsides—even on slag heaps and pit banks in industrial counties.

It is the shape of coltsfoot leaves, often 150 mm (6 in.) across, which gives the plant its English name. The Latin name, *Tussilago farfara*, means cough plant—the Romans used coltsfoot and related species of herbs as cough cures. Lowland Scots call the plant tussiligi and they too use it to relieve coughs.

To use: Coltsfoot leaves are unsuitable as a vegetable but should be brewed in water to make a spring tonic. Or—a real money

saver this—dried, cut and smoked. I do not claim it is like Virginia tobacco exactly, but if needs be a taste for a pipeful can be acquired. (Time was, I recall from my long ago BBC days, when a very senior announcer was in the habit of smoking coltsfoot blended with a little dried lavender for delicate aroma!)

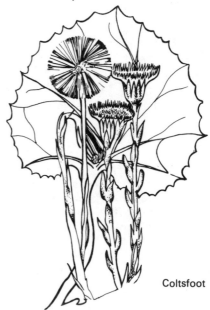

Coltsfoot

Local names: Baccy plant, Somerset; clatterclogs, Cumberland; cleat, Yorkshire and Lincolnshire; dummyleaf, Hertfordshire; and foal's foot in many parts of the Midlands and North.

Common sorrel

One of the most common—and earliest to appear—grassland plants in the country. *Rumex acetosa* grows about 0.6 m (2 ft.) high, has arrow-shaped leaves and tall spikes of dock-like flowers (a very different plant from the delicate little wood sorrel—see Salads section, p. 28).

Like cleavers, its leaves can be picked as early as February, and in France this sorrel is a valued vegetable. Cook the leaves as you would spinach, or use them chopped and mixed with onion to make sorrel soup.

Common sorrel

Broad-leaved Dock

Green sauce is a familiar local name for common sorrel in many parts of the country, presumably from the fact that the plant was formerly much used to prepare a green sauce for fish.

Dock

There are two varieties of the familiar dock: the broad-leaved dock (*Rumex obstusifolius*), which children often rub on nettle stings, and curled dock (*R. crispus*). Docks are troublesome weeds everywhere, but curled dock with its crinkly leaves can be used (when very young) cooked with bacon or ham. Broad-leaved dock was formerly used to wrap farmhouse butter and keep it fresh.

Golden saxifrage

There are quite a number of saxifrages, little plants which creep and climb among rocks and mountains (and, of course, the cultivated species of the domestic rock

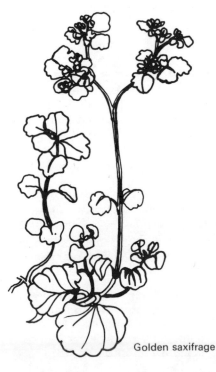

Golden saxifrage

garden). The first plant, *Saxifraga miralis*, was found in North Wales in 1639 and it took botanists another 200 years to find a dozen species—the last, *Saxifraga cespitosa*, again in Wales.

Golden saxifrage (*Chrysosplenium oppositifolium*), a little plant of wet, shady places, forms a dense mat of rooting stems. As its name implies, it has yellow flowers and is fairly common in the North and West. In Wiltshire it is called buttered eggs. An exception to the rock habitat of the saxifrages is the meadow saxifrage, an increasingly rare white-flowered plant of old meadows and permanent pastures in lowland Britain.

To eat: The leaves of the golden saxifrage grow as a rosette beneath the groups of petal-less flowers, and can be used as a green vegetable, cooked in a little boiling water. Or, as in the Vosges area of eastern France (where it is called cresson de roche), it can be eaten fresh in a salad.

Shepherd's purse

This is so named because the heart-shaped seed pods of this annual resemble the type of purse carried by shepherds in the Middle Ages.

Although it is very plentiful in these early months of the year its white flowers can, in fact, be seen in every month of the year (so can gorse—hence the old gibe that a country lass could only permit kissing during months when the gorse was in bloom!)

Shepherd's purse, Latin name *Capsella bursa-pastoris*, grows in waste places and arable fields in almost every country in the world and it can be recognised by its rosette of leaves pressed very close to the ground.

To eat: Use the chopped leaves like cabbage. It was formerly widely used as a herb to relieve inflammation; also, a cloth steeped in shepherd's purse juice was put up the nose to stop bleeding.

Local names: Bad man's oatmeal, Durham; gentlemen's purse, Somerset; lady's purses, East Anglia; blindweed, and pick-pocket-to-London, Yorkshire; pick-pocket, in many midland and southern

Shepherd's purse

counties. And, perhaps the oddest of many other local names for shepherd's purse, in Warwickshire my family used to call it naughty man's plaything.

April–May

With the coming of spring and more sunshine these months are very prolific in wild flowers and plants, many of which are good to eat though so few people seem to realise this.

Beech

This colourful giant is a native tree and among our most beautiful. Although beech, *Fagus sylvatica*, does not reproduce naturally north of the Midlands and South Wales because it needs warm summers to ripen its seeds, it has been planted throughout the country. Gilbert White wrote of the beeches around Selborne, 'the most lovely of all fruit trees, whether we consider its smooth rind or bark, its glossy foliage, or graceful pendulous branches'.

Beech is easy to identify from the smooth, grey bark and slender zigzag twigs carrying thin, pointed brown-scaled buds. The leaves are a translucent pale green in spring, dark green in summer and golden-brown before the fall. The finest beech

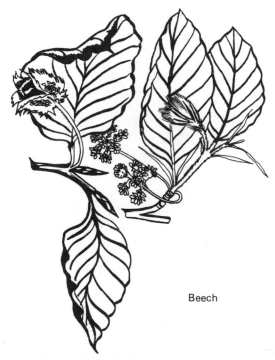

Beech

trees grow on chalk, for instance in the Cotswolds, on the South Downs and in Buckinghamshire (a place name derived from the Old English word *bece*, meaning beech) where the furniture industry was founded on the Chiltern beechwoods.

To eat: Fresh from the tree in spring, beech leaves—they are silky to the touch and tear easily—make a fine, sweet salad vegetable; or the young leaves can be cooked as a green vegetable.

To drink: Much more exciting is to make a liqueur called beech-leaf noyau, thought to have originated in the Chilterns.

Pack an earthenware or glass jar almost full with young beech leaves and pour on gin, pressing the leaves down until just covered with the gin. Leave for a couple of weeks; next strain off the by then brilliant green-coloured gin and to every pint add up to a pound of sugar—depending on how syrupy you wish the liqueur to be—dissolved in half a pint of boiling water. Finally, add a little brandy, mix well and bottle up when cold.

You will find beech-leaf noyau sweet, slightly oily and very potent. You have been warned!

The triangular brown nuts are often called beech-mast and it forms a staple part of the autumn and winter diet of much wild life—including squirrels, mice, jays, pheasants, tits and other small birds. Years ago beech-mast was valued as pig food and New Forest commoners still drive their pigs into the woodlands for this purpose.

Charlock

As a weed in cornfields this plant is a big nuisance to farmers. Its seeds can remain buried under grass for up to half a century—then germinate when the land is ploughed.

Between 0.3 and 0.6 m (1 and 2 ft.) tall, charlock, Latin name *Sinapis arvensis*, has broadly toothed, lyre-shaped leaves. The bright yellow, four-petalled flowers are followed by angular fruit pods containing a row of dark brown seeds.

To eat: Despite a bitter flavour, the leaves of charlock can be used as spinach—indeed were sold as such in Dublin in times gone by.

Local names: Bazzocks, wild turnip and runch, in Yorkshire and Northumberland; cadlock or carlock in most midland

Charlock

inns and road fords—places where horse travellers were expected to arrive with, or suffer, broken bones!

Old herbalists praise the juice of comfrey leaves picked in summer as 'most healing for those bursten within', and indeed it was a country custom to drink it to alleviate pleurisy or gastric ulcer. Washes of fresh comfrey juice are also claimed to promote quick skin growth over abrasions.

Comfrey

counties; wild mustard or yellow weed, Cumberland and Scotland; and zenry in Somerset.

Comfrey

Colonies of this large, bushy plant are often seen along river banks and roadside ditches. The drooping, bell-like flowers of comfrey (Latin name *Symphytum officinale*) have differing colours, ranging from pale yellow to purple and violet. (It is useless to pick the attractive flowers since they shrivel up immediately.)

In Scotland, still called 'boneset', it has long been used as a medium for setting bones and as a plaster to prevent wounds shrinking in healing—in fact, this most interesting plant has never been taken out of the *British Pharmacopoeia*. It is the root, lifted in spring and containing a glutinous, slimy juice which sets solid, that is used as a plaster or poultice.

Comfrey, growing up to 1 m (3 ft.) high, is frequently found around old coaching

To eat: The leaves of comfrey are dull in colour and hairy underneath; use like spinach, but with plenty of seasoning. The furriness of the leaves disappears with cooking.

I have not myself tried it but Richard Mabey, in his book *Food for Free*, considers the best recipe to be a German fritter called Schwarzwarz which is made by leaving the stalks on the comfrey leaves which are dipped in a thin batter and then fried in deep fat for about two minutes.

Local names: In the West Country the plant is called church bells, and coffee flower. In Lincolnshire—Abraham, Isaac and Joseph.

Good King Henry

This wild plant has the distinction of having been introduced, in Roman times, as a vegetable from central Europe. The name itself came from Germany where Henry, or Heinrich, is an elf-name for a woodland creature. What is more, the name Good King Henry for the plant known botanically as *Chenopodium bonus-henricus* distinguishes it from Bad Henry, or Böser Heinrich, the evil goblin, which is the German name for a poisonous plant we know as dog's mercury (*Mercurialis perennis*).

Good King Henry

Found by roadsides and around old buildings throughout Britain, Good King Henry is a spinach-like plant with broad spear-shaped leaves and spikes of very small greenish-yellow flowers—these flower clusters are mostly at the end of the stem.

To eat: Both the young shoots and flowering tops can be boiled and eaten with butter. Or the young leaves can be used as a salad ingredient. I cannot honestly say that the flavour of this wild vegetable is very special despite its once being called English All Good and being cultivated in the North as a pot herb.

Local names: In Shropshire they call it Johnny O'Neale, in Lincolnshire it becomes feminine—Margery. Parts of the South Country confuse the issue by naming it fat hen whereas this is the popular name for a separate plant (*Chenopodium album*, see page 20). There are many other picturesque local names for the plant, including shoemaker's heels, in Shropshire and parts of mid-Wales; good neighbourhood, in Wiltshire; and midden mylies in Scotland.

Ground elder

A great nuisance to the gardener, with its white, thread-like roots going deep down in the soil, this weed is useful when eaten like spinach. It has a spicy flavour.

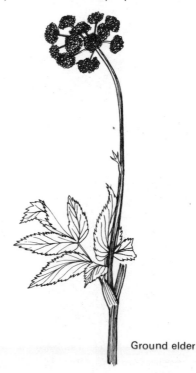

Ground elder

The plant (Latin name *Aegopodium podagraria*) was introduced in the Middle Ages as a pot-herb and a medicine against gout—an alternative name being goutweed.

Local names: Goat's foot, Devon; jack-jump-about, in several Midland counties; and ashweed in parts of the South Country.

Hogweed

A plant often called cow parsnip and found in hedgerows, open woods and grassy places throughout the country (Latin name, *Heracleum sphondylium*). It has rough, hairy and grooved hollow stems and grows up to 1.8 m (6 ft.) tall, with white flowers.

It must on no account be confused with another tall plant with hollow stems, white flowers in early summer and with a name also beginning with the letter H. This plant, hemlock (*Conium maculatum*), is very poisonous—and was so used by the

Greeks and Romans. But it has a smooth (not grooved as hogweed) purple-spotted stem, an unpleasant smell and round fruits as distinct from hogweed whose seeds are flat. Hemlock's leaves, more feathery than those of hogweed, produce a sedative drug.

To eat: Not only is hogweed widely used as pig food, the young leaves can also be used as a green vegetable. In his 1899 *English Botany*, Sowerby says that the sprouting leaves and shoots 'taste like asparagus'.

Local names: There are scores of names for this plant, but here is a selection—bear's breech. or bilders, in the West Country; broad elk or bunwort, Yorkshire and Scotland; cushia, North Country; devil's oatmeal and gipsy's lace in Warwickshire and Somerset respectively; keck or kesh, over widely separated parts of the country; similarly widespread over several counties is the country name rabbit's meat for hogweed.

Jack-by-the-hedge

This is, in fact, garlic mustard and grows in hedge banks up to 1.2 m (4 ft.) high with heart-shaped leaves having very distinct veins. When these leaves are crushed, or if you smell the roots, they give off a strong smell of garlic. The pure white flowers of this wild mustard (Latin name, *Alliaria petiolata*) were once valued in making a sauce for salt fish, and in Somerset the plant was known as 'sauce alone'.

Incidentally, the popular name Jack-by-the-hedge (or sometimes Jack-in-the-hedge) is in certain localities given to quite a different plant—red campion, which is not edible in any way. All the mustard plants—and there are several, including black, white, hedge and treacle—are so named for the condiment prepared from the seeds of the cultivated black and white mustard plants.

To eat: Probably best to use the leaves as garlic flavouring for salads or sauces

Hogweed

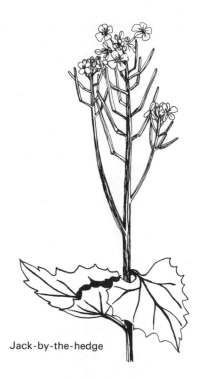

Jack-by-the-hedge

although the Victorian garden writer, J. C. Loudon, in his *Encyclopaedia of Gardening* (1848 edn) referred to its use as a boiled vegetable pleasant to eat with boiled mutton.

Local names: Beggarman's oatmeal, Leicestershire; lady's needlework or lamb's pummy, Somerset; poor man's mustard, Lincolnshire.

Lungwort

The name comes from the supposed likeness—at least to our forefathers—of the white spotted leaves to human lungs, and earlier generations thought its appearance was a sign that the plant could cure respiratory diseases such as tuberculosis, pneumonia and bronchitis.

The plant (Latin name, *Pulmonaria officinalis*) was introduced to Britain from Central Europe and cultivated in gardens. It grows up to 0.3 m (1 ft.) high in woods and hedgerows. The flowers are at first

pink then turn blue. This colour change accounts for the alternative double names —Adam and Eve, Joseph and Mary— although these are usually given to the much rarer variety of narrow-leaved lungwort, *Pulmonaria longifolia*.

Lungwort

To eat: Use the leaves as a green vegetable.

Local names: Jerusalem cowslip, in many parts of the country; bottle-of-all-sorts, Cumberland; the Good Friday plant, Somerset; lady's pin-cushion, Cheshire and Yorkshire; spotted virgin, Herefordshire; Virgin Mary's milkdrops, Wiltshire; and the variation Virgin Mary's tears, in Dorset.

Red valerian

Introduced from southern Europe in the sixteenth century, this attractive plant (Latin name, *Kentranthus ruber*) has become naturalised throughout the country on old walls, cliffs and quarries, to which its downy seeds are easily spread by the wind. There is also a white-flowered variety and two other species known as marsh valerian (*Valeriana dioica*) and common valerian (*Valeriana officinalis*), a pink flowered plant—with an unpleasant smell —usually found in damp and shady places throughout the British Isles.

The edible variety, red valerian, with which we are concerned in this book, grows 0.6 m to 0.9 m (2 ft. to 3 ft.) tall and is interesting on account of having its flowers pollinated by butterflies.

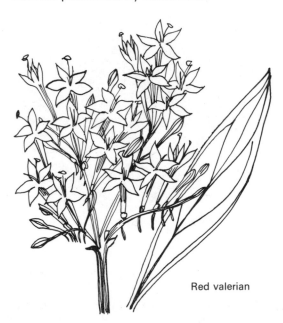

Red valerian

I often wondered why my wife, who spent her childhood in Somerset and Devon, always called valerian 'drunkards' —until I read Geoffrey Grigson's description of the plant: 'Blowing a little drunkenly in the wind, how fine it is on the limestone walls of Plymouth', and further inquiries showed that in Somerset and Devon popular local names for valerian are drunkards, drunkard's nose, drunken Willy and drunken sailor.

To eat: Very young leaves of red valerian are commonly eaten in salads in France and Italy, although slightly bitter to the taste. You may prefer to boil the leaves and shake them up with butter. Gerard mentioned the 'excellent sweete savour of the roots'.

Local names: Like several others in my book the plant has acquired a fascinating list of popular names, besides the 'drunkards' of the West Country, and these include: in Lincolnshire, cat bed and German laycock (i.e. lilac); kiss-me-quick, Dorset and Wiltshire; and pretty Betsy in the South Country.

Spring beauty

This was the name the Americans gave to a white-flowered variety of pink purslane (*Claytonia alsinoides*) which was not observed in this country until the mid nineteenth century.

It is a smooth, fleshy annual growing about 0.3 m (1 ft.) high, locally common

Spring beauty

on sandy waste land. The plant has its stem leaves joined together so that the stem appears to go through the middle of the leaf.

To eat: Spring beauty is tender and succulent and best boiled like spinach.

Strawberry

Though small, the fruits of the wild straw-berry (*Fragaria vesca*) are well worth pick-ing to eat fresh with sugar and cream, or to make into jam (they are sweeter than the

Strawberry

garden strawberry). However, the plant comes into this book because its furry-tasting leaves can also be cooked as a green vegetable.

Wild strawberry is found in scrub, open woods and hedges throughout the British Isles, particularly on lime-rich soils.

Yarrow

Blooming throughout our summer, this is one of the commonest of all wild flowers—especially by roadsides. The second part of its scientific name *Achillea millefolium* means literally 'thousand leaf' and refers to the familiar feathery leaves. An alternative name for the plant is milfoil. The flowers can be white, pink and occasionally purple, and have a strong aromatic smell.

Yarrow

Apart from its culinary uses, yarrow has the property of stopping bleeding and was formerly so used as a wound-herb, as well as a tonic and for treating heavy colds. On St John's Eve the Irish hang yarrow in their homes to avert illness.

Take the leaves of yarrow off the tough stems and boil as a vegetable.

Local names: Woundwort, in Somerset; thousand-leaf grass, Staffordshire; hem-ming-and-sowing, Hampshire; sneeze-wort, Gloucestershire; traveller's ease, Wiltshire; and old man's mustard, Lincolnshire.

June–July

Bistort

A North Country plant this, or at least it is more frequently seen there—often in big circular patches of bright reddish-white flowers in old meadows near villages.

The botanical name of the plant, which has distorted underground stems, is *Polygonum bistorta*—derived from the Latin *bis*, twice, and *tortus*, twisted. An alternative general name for bistort is snakeweed, also because of its twisted underground stems.

Bistort grows about 0.6 m (2 ft.) high, its pink spikes topping off a straight, hairless stem. The leaves are triangular or arrow shaped, on long stalks. Look for it in

Bistort

wet, hilly pastures—except in the South—for it certainly makes a fine display.

The tradition of eating bistort continues in the North Country. Richard Mabey, in his *Food for Free*, recalls that in the spring of 1971 the following advertisement appeared in the Personal Column of *The Times*: 'Polygonum bistorta—How is your Dock Pudding?' Entrants were sought for the first World Championship Dock Pudding Contest, in the Calder Valley in Yorkshire (gentle dock, or passion dock, are midland and northern names for bistort). There were over fifty entries from the one valley alone!

To eat: In the Lake District the young leaves are an important ingredient of Easter Ledge Pudding, usually eaten with veal and for which there are many recipes. Mabey gives this one from Westmorland:

Gather a good quantity of mixed spring leaves, mainly bistort, but also young nettle tops, dandelion leaves and lady's mantle (*Alchemilla vulgaris*, prized in the sixteenth century when bandages were dipped in its juice to heal wounds). Boil in water for ten minutes, strain and chop the leaves. Next add one beaten egg, one hard-boiled egg chopped small, butter, salt and pepper—and mix well into the leaves. Put back in the saucepan, heat through and then transfer to a hot pudding basin to shape.

Local names: Apart from being called gentle or passion dock in Nottinghamshire, Derbyshire and Yorkshire, bistort is called adderwort in Somerset; Easter giant and Easter ledges in Cumberland and Yorkshire; poor man's cabbage, Lancashire; red legs, Warwickshire and Shropshire.

Fat hen

A common wild plant, the leaves of which were used as food from prehistoric time but is now largely regarded only as a nuisance weed. The black, shiny seeds have a high fat and albumen content and were also eaten, with other grain—the seeds have been identified from the Bronze Age in Sussex and Scotland.

The plant *Chenopodium album* is sometimes called wild spinach and it was after the introduction of spinach to Britain from south-west Asia that fat hen lost its importance as a green vegetable.

William Curtis, in his *Flora Londinensis* (1771–91), refers to the gathering of fat hen from dunghills and gardens, warning readers not to pick *Solanum nigrum*, or black nightshade, by mistake. This poisonous plant, found in hedges and damp woodlands, belongs to the same family as the potato and tomato. Its small green or

Fat hen

black berries are less likely to attract children than the large black, cherry-like berries of deadly nightshade (*Atropa belladonna*—the latter part of this name being that of the drug derived from this dangerous plant, all parts of which can kill).

Fat hen is found on wasteland and in arable fields everywhere. It grows 0.9 m (3 ft.) high and its triangular-shaped leaves are often covered with a white, mealy substance. Its distinctive spikes carry clusters of inconspicuous small green flowers.

To eat: This is certainly one of the more valuable wild foods since, besides the fat and albumen content of fat hen leaves already mentioned, they are rich in vitamins and iron. The leaves should be used like spinach—very good with bacon as well as with meat.

During my boyhood in Warwickshire, a few of the cottagers made fritters with fat hen leaves. The ingredients were a pound of leaves, one egg, soft breadcrumbs and seasoning—plus grated nutmeg. After

cooking the wild spinach (which thereabouts fat hen was always called) it was chopped and strained, the other ingredients added and shaped into small flat cakes before frying in very hot fat.

Local names: Fat hen is the most generally used popular name, but bacon weed in Dorset; dungweed or dirtweed, in the south Midlands; muckweed in eastern counties and Yorkshire.

Hop

The hop plant (*Humulus lupulus*) was originally a native of wet woods in southern England and was first taken in cultivation in the early sixteenth century for flavouring beer. Now, it can be found climbing in hedges throughout Britain.

Beer is originally a northern drink, but the word hop and the art of flavouring beer with the female flowers of this plant we took from the Netherlands and, as Geoffrey Grigson has reminded us (roughly true but not absolutely accurate)—

Hops, Reformation, bays and beer
Came to England all in one year.

Gerard wrote in 1597: 'the manifold vertues in Hops (cleansing and opening the body, purging the blood etc.) do manifestly argue the holsomnesse of Beere above Ale; for the Hops rather make it a Phisicall drinke to help the body in health, then an ordinarie drinke for the quenching of our thirst'.

In spring, the hop plant sends up thin, twining stems which grow rapidly. Both these stems and the leaves have a rough surface. There are both male and female plants and it is the female flowers, developed into the greenish-yellow cones covered in resinous glands, which the brewers use not only to give beer its bitter tang but also to clarify it and help the beer to keep longer.

To eat: In Kent, where I for a time studied and wrote about the commercial growing of hops, an appetising local dish consists

Hop

Nettle

There are two nettles which sting. The big one, which grows up to 1.5 m (5 ft.) tall and is common throughout Britain, is the stinging nettle (Latin name, *Urtica dioica*); the smaller or annual nettle (*Urtica urena*) which grows only to about 0.6 m (2 ft.) is also common, but not in western areas.

In the Highlands and Islands nettles were thought to grow from the bodies of dead men, a myth arising perhaps because nettles are prolific where man has previously cultivated and enriched the soil, leaving behind him traces of former dwellings. In Denmark nettles are said to mark the homes of elves.

Unlike so many edible plants mentioned in this book, the nettle does not appear to have any extensive folklore of popular or local names—except for devil's leaf and devil's plaything. The stinging hairs of the nettle have a pointed single cell above a bulbous base holding a poisonous liquid, formic acid. The hairs are brittle and, after

of the tops of hop plants cut in spring, boiled in broth and eaten like asparagus with buttered toast.

Hop sauce is another Kentish speciality. For this you gather young shoots (only about four leaves down from the top) not later than May and lay them to soak in cold water with a handful of salt. Next drain, plunge into boiling water and boil rapidly until tender. Pour off the water instantly (says Dorothy Hartley, whom I have to thank for the recipe) and chop into a plain butter sauce. Serve with fish, chicken or instead of caper sauce with mutton.

Hop shoots have long been extensively used as a green vegetable, but they also make a good soup. For this, another recipe from Dorothy Hartley's *Food in England* (1954) suggests using the dried peas of winter to make a thick pea soup into which you tip a double handful of finely chopped hop tops and cook gently until soft. Then add a little scraped onion, pepper and salt, and—just before serving—a cupful of milk.

Nettle

piercing the skin, they break off and irritation follows the formic acid entering the pierced skin.

However, despite its stinging nuisance, the nettle is a valuable wild plant. Before cotton was imported, the fibres in the stems of nettles were spun and made into cloth for sheets and tablecloths. During the last war many tons of nettles were gathered for the extraction of chlorophyll and of dyes for camouflage nets.

To eat: Certainly the best-known use for young nettle tops is to cook the leaves like spinach—do not pick later than June (unless from new young plants), as when the leaves are coarse in texture they taste bitter and are a strong laxative.

Nettle soup is good. Boil the leaves gently as for spinach then press through a sieve. Melt an ounce of butter in a pan and into this stir the same quantity of flour. Add salt and pepper. Next take this from the stove and add a pint of milk, beating until the mixture is smooth. Boil this up and simmer for five minutes, stirring the mixture, after which this is poured on to the nettle purée and mixed well.

Nettle tea is brewed from the dried leaves (in fact these dried leaves can still be bought for making this herbal tea) and another wholesome drink is nettle beer. For the following recipe I have to thank a lady in a Worcestershire village where my mother's family were farmers:

Wash 2 gallons by measure of young nettles and put into a saucepan with 2 gallons of water, $\frac{1}{2}$ oz. of root ginger, 4 lb. of malt, 2 oz. of hops and 4 oz. of sarsaparilla (all these can usually be obtained at a good dispensing chemist's shop although the sarsaparilla—the dried root of a South American plant used both for flavouring and as a root beer—may be scarce).

Boil for a quarter of an hour; put $1\frac{1}{2}$ lb. of castor sugar into a large pan or earthenware jar and strain the nettle mixture on to it. This must now be stirred until the sugar has dissolved. Beat 1 oz. of yeast (a working baker's shop is the most likely source for this) to a cream and add this, leaving until it begins to ferment. Finally, put into bottles, cork and tie down with string. Nettle beer does not need keeping—you can drink it at once.

Rosebay willow-herb

Named after its narrow, willow-like leaves, this plant grows as an upright spike up to 1.2 m (4 ft.) high covered with purplish flowers.

It spreads and colonises waste places very quickly. Rosebay willow-herb (*Epilobium angustifolium*), the only one of eight willow-herbs we are concerned with, was a rare native species which suddenly began to spread about 1860 and is now

Rosebay willow-herb

common everywhere (except the west of Ireland) probably partly because its thousands of cottony seeds blow away easily in the wind and, botanists think, because of some genetic change.

Rosebay willow-herb loves to grow on ground where there has been a fire and its popular name is fireweed—originally so described in the West Country.

To eat: Use the green leaves, whilst still young, as a green vegetable. And, according to Carl Linnaeus, the eighteenth-century Swedish botanist to whom we owe the definition of the world's plant species, the young shoots of rosebay willow-herb can be served like asparagus.

Local names: Apple-pie, Somerset; cat's eyes, Shropshire; ranting widow, Cheshire; and in Ireland, blooming Sally.

Wild beet

This common seashore plant (*Beta vulgaris*) is the wild ancestor of beetroot, sugar beet and mangold. It grows about 0.6 m (2 ft.) tall and the large lower leaves often form a rosette at the base of the plant, then get smaller as they grow up the stem. The flowers are insignificant, greenish-white in colour.

Seakale is also an edible seashore plant but a different species altogether (see under Stems for Cooking, p. 51).

Cultivation of wild beet is thought to have been started by the Persians who valued the plant for its sturdy roots which anchored it in the sands of the Mediterranean and Caspian Seas. Through centuries of cultivation, selection and ac-

Wild beet

cidental crossing there has evolved a group of plants of very considerable importance in the agricultural economy (incidentally it was the Germans in the eighteenth century who first noticed the sugar in beetroot).

To eat: The leaves of wild beet (sometimes called sea spinach) can be used as a vegetable, soup base or tart filling.

2. Leaves for Salads

March–April

Rightly prominent in this section of the book, and among the earliest of our edible wild plants to flower is the ubiquitous and oft-despised dandelion—but it is, in fact, one of the most useful of all the plants I deal with since the leaves can be eaten not only in salads but also used as a vegetable, along with the roots. The plant gives us a further bonus as a fresh food for the domestic rabbit and neither should we forget dandelion drinks.

This section also includes another of the most familiar of all wild plants to generations of children—wood sorrel, a 'magic' plant with leaves like shamrock and about which folklore abounds in many parts of Europe as well as in this country.

The plants in this section are almost exclusively used in salads—certain others, whose secondary use is salad, appeared in Section 1, as Leaves for Cooking.

Corn salad

Corn salad

Often called lamb's lettuce, this small annual is a common plant of fields, railway banks and hedges, especially on dry soil. Corn salad (*Valerianella locusta*) has pale blue or lilac flowers and a three-chambered seed pod in which two of the compartments are always empty, but I don't know why!

Appearing before early lettuce in our gardens, the long and narrow leaves of corn salad can be eaten in salads.

Dandelion

The name of the plant is a corruption of the French 'dent de lion', meaning lion's tooth—but it is not known whether this refers to the long root of the dandelion plant, to the toothed leaves or to parts of the bright yellow flowers.

Of all its many alternative names the commonest is clock, or fairy clocks, one o'clock and what o'clock, and this arises from the ages-old children's custom of puffing away the round, white seed-heads—the number of puffs required to dispel all the seed 'parachutes' supposedly telling the time.

The dandelion has a few medicinal traditions, being diuretic and cleansing. Country children (myself included years ago!) warn each other against picking dandelions because 'they make you wet the bed'. The

Dandelion

The flowers, about a three-quart measure, must be freshly gathered, picked off their stalks and put into a gallon of water. Bring the water to the boil, pour over the dandelions and leave in a muslin-covered bowl for three days—stirring each day. Next add 3 lb. of sugar and the rinds of two lemons and an orange, turn it all into a pan and boil up for an hour.

Stage two is to put the brew back into the bowl, adding the pulp from the lemons and the orange from which you removed the rind. When cool, add an ounce of yeast and again leave covered for three days—when the dandelion wine will be ready to strain and bottle up.

Do not quite fill the bottles since the product is improved by the addition of a pound of raisins—equally divided among the bottles. Leave corking loose until fermentation ceases.

This wine, made in May or June, is good at Christmas.

Local names: There are scores of variations in different parts of the country and, apart from the very familiar ones I have already mentioned, they include devil's milk pail and lay a-bed, Somerset; dindle, East Anglia; dog-posy and pissimire, the Lake District and Yorkshire; wet weed, Wiltshire; witch gowan, Scotland; and canker in Gloucestershire.

Hairy bittercress

This is one of three types of bittercress, but as it is only slightly hairy it is not well named (Latin name, *Cardamine hirsuta*). Its relatives are large bittercress, usually found in wet areas, and the shade-loving wavy or wood bittercress of the streamside. All three are edible.

Hairy bittercress occurs in drier places and is a common garden weed, sometimes confused with the larger shepherd's purse plant—both have their leaves mostly at the base.

The leaves taste rather like watercress and are agreeably bitter used in salads.

name 'piss-a-bed' is studiously ignored by polite adults here though the French version 'pissenlit' is, typically, acceptable!

Dandelion roots contain a milky juice, once used by medicine men for liver complaints and in the last war the root was dried and used as a substitute for chicory and coffee (see p. 30).

There are more than a hundred species of dandelion adapted to differing local conditions, the common one being *Taraxacum officinale*. An interesting variety is the lesser dandelion (*T. laevigatum*), adapted to growing in very dry places.

To eat: The blanched leaves make a bitter flavoured addition to salads. The leaves can also be braised as a vegetable, and the roots, cut into thin slices, are good when cooked in a little stock until tender.

The flowers of the dandelion make a popular home wine, for which I have this recipe from Cheshire:

Hairy bittercress

Hawthorn

Lady's smock

Hawthorn

Since the flowers and fruits of this widespread bush have so many culinary uses it is very fully described in the companion volume to this book, *Wild Fruits and Nuts*. However, it must be listed here, as hawthorn leaves, picked in April, are an excellent, nutty-flavoured addition to salads.

Lady's smock

Another plant in the *Cardamine* group (see hairy bittercress p. 26), this is popularly called cuckoo flower since it comes into flower when the cuckoo is first heard. The Latin name of this most delightful lilac-coloured flower of wet meadows and marshland is *Cardamine pratensis*.

Geoffrey Grigson has an interesting explanation for the name lady's smock. In Old English 'smick' was another word for smock and 'smickering', or to 'smicker' were, says this writer, words for amorous looks and purposes. 'Smock' was used coarsely in the sixteenth century, rather like today's phrase 'a piece of skirt'.

Another theory maintains that it is so named because the large patches of flowers are occasionally white, resembling linen bleaching in the sun.

It is traditionally unlucky, and not only in the United Kingdom, to pick cuckoo flowers for the house. In Germany it is called a donnerblume, a gewitterblume or a thunder and storm flower, and is not to be picked and brought indoors for fear of the home being struck by lightning: the French also give the elegant lady's smock a similar association—fleur de tonnerre.

Common throughout the British Isles, lady's smock leaves are a good substitute for watercress in salad.

Local names: Apple pie, bog-flower or bird's eye, Yorkshire; cuckoo bread, West Country; cuckoo-pint in several counties, including Leicestershire; lady's flock, Nottinghamshire; lucky locket, Derbyshire and the former county of Rutland; milk maids, in many parts of the country.

Wood sorrel

A familiar and delicate little plant this, growing in woods and shady places all through the kingdom. Several of its common names are shared with common sorrel (*Rumex acetosa*) which is described on page 10.

The edible wood sorrel (*Oxalis acetosella*) is easily recognised by its white flowers and shamrock-shaped leaves—folded to begin with—on a plant no higher than about 100 mm (4 in.). The folding leaves explain the plant sometimes being known as sleeping beauty, or sleeping clover.

For over five hundred years wood sorrel has been used as a salad vegetable, and after John Evelyn at the end of the seventeenth century recommended it as a plant for kitchen gardens, wood sorrel was cultivated for use in salads and sauces. Rich-

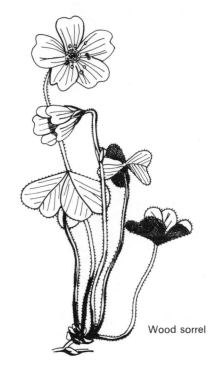

Wood sorrel

ard Mabey mentions that the American Indians used to use the roots of wood sorrel to increase the speed of their horses.

To eat: Either use the sharp-tasting leaves as a salad ingredient, cooked like spinach, or as sorrel sauce. However, use wood sorrel leaves sparingly owing to their content of oxalic acid salts.

Sorrel salad was once much favoured with lamb or veal cutlets; sorrel sauce goes with duckling, goose and rabbit.

John Simpson, in his *Complete System of Cookery* (1806), gives this recipe for sorrel and orange sauce—but you might find it necessary to add quite a lot of sugar to please today's tastes:

Chop about four large handfuls of sorrel. Put into a stewpan with a small piece of butter, a slice of ham and two onions chopped fine. Put them on the fire to simmer for half an hour then rub it through a tammy [i.e. a sieve] and add a little coulis [thick brown stock] to it. Squeeze a lemon and Seville orange if to be had—if not, two lemons, a little pepper and salt, and sugar to make it palatable.

Sorrel is still much liked on the Continent. Here is how to make green sorrel sauce:

Wash a pound of sorrel, and remove the stalks. Place in a pan without any more water than that clinging to it, and cook over a fierce heat for five minutes—turning it so the top leaves can also cook in their own juice as does spinach.

Press the cooked sorrel through a sieve into a pan with an ounce of unsalted butter, two tablespoonsful of thick cream, one teaspoonful of sugar and its own liquid. Let it simmer for three or four minutes until very hot. If the sauce is too thick, a little stock may be added.

Local names: Bread-and-cheese, Devon and Somerset; cuckoo flower, in many areas; king-fisher, Buckinghamshire; rabbit's food, Lancashire; sour grass and woodsour, Yorkshire.

May–June

By now spring has given way to early summer and it is in these two months that we can go out and find the greatest variety of edible wild leaves for use in green salads starting, at least alphabetically for the purposes of this book, with brooklime which has little blue flowers like a forget-me-not and can be used as watercress—but is easier to find. However, perhaps the most versatile free harvest during these months is wintergreen (*Pyrola minor*), found mainly in the North Country—its leaves can be used not only in salads but, in dried form, as a substitute for tea.

Several others of our wild plants are, in fact, suitable for making substitute tea—including borage, catmint, chamomile, burnet, clover, meadowsweet, nettle, heather, elderflower, tansy, yarrow—and the blossoms of the lime tree. Just as ordinary teas are made by blending different species, so a refreshing tea can be brewed from experimenting with the flowers and leaves of any of the plants just mentioned. With tea as expensive as it is these days, free home-blended tea is quite a thought!

To dry flowers and leaves for tea, pick them in fine weather and when the flowers are in full bloom. Remove any dirt and rubbish (but do not wash as this spoils the texture and flavour) and spread out on a tray to dry. To brew, or mash, the tea is easy—just pour boiling water into a jug over the flowers and leaves, let it stand for a short while then strain off the liquid.

Brooklime

This is a water speedwell and, unlike its relative, common speedwell, which likes dry grasslands, is found in ponds, streams and muddy places with its creeping stems rooting or floating in water.

The Latin name is *Veronica beccabunga* and, like the other seven species of speedwell, it has attractive small blue flowers on fairly long stalks. Its fleshy leaves grow in

Brooklime

pairs, opposite each other on the stem, and were long recommended against scurvy.

To eat: Following the example of northern Europe where it is used just like watercress, you will find brooklime leaves and the young tops of the plant quite pleasant in a salad—even if a little bitter.

Local names: Horse-cress, in Yorkshire; pig's grease, Dorset; cow-cress, Devon; and Devonians also call it becey leaves.

Cat's ear

Without any doubt, this is one of the most common wild flowers of meadows and grass verges throughout Britain. It has yellow, dandelion-like flowers but is a big plant—up to 0.6 m (2 ft.) tall—with branched flowering stems which are leafless.

Incidentally, you may be surprised to learn just how many wild plants are commonly called 'cat's' this or that—for instance, cat's claws; cat's clover; cat's eye; cat's face; cat's foot; cat's love; cat's milk; cat's paw; cat's peas and cat's tails!

Cat's ear

Common cat's ear (*Hypochoeris radicata*) is but one of the same family which includes the dandelion and all can be used in salads. Others include chicory, nipplewort, hawkbit, goat's-beard and corn sow thistle, and these are all described in this section of the book, according to their season.

Chicory

This plant, the flowers of which are a light and beautiful blue, is very local in England and Wales—usually one finds it on chalky soil—and rare in Scotland. It grows up to 0.9 m (3 ft.) tall and has hairy leaves on tough, furrowed stems. One German book

Chicory

on folklore explains how a young girl would only stop weeping for her dead lover when she was turned into a flower by the roadside—and so she became the Wegwort, or chicory.

The leaves of chicory (Latin name *Cichorium intybus*) can be used as a salad ingredient (incidentally, the cultivated version is called endive). Its roots can be dried and ground to make a coffee substitute.

Like other blue flowers, including bluebells, chicory turns red through the acid of ants if placed in an ant hill. Medically, chicory used to be considered good for purging and for the bladder.

Goat's beard

The dandelion-like fruiting 'clock' of this climbing plant is familiar along our lanes and in rough grassland everywhere except in the West. The flowers are, however, seen only in the mornings, because they close at mid-day—hence the common names Jack-go-to-bed-at-noon, or sometimes, sleep-at-noon.

The name goat's beard (Latin, *Tragopogon pratensis*) refers to the long, silky 'parachute' hairs which appear when the flower reopens and are designed to help blow the seed away in the wind.

A very similar species, but with purple flowers, is salsify (*T. porrifolius*), oc-

casionally found as an escapee from gardens, often near the sea.

Goat's beard leaves are used in salads, and its roots used also to be eaten. Somerset people have two pleasant popular names for the plant—sleepy head, and twelve o'clocks.

Hawkbit

As a family of common plants, the hawkbits have yellow flowers on fairly tall leafless stems. Hawkbits are common everywhere, but the edible one—called rough hawkbit (*Leontodon hispidus*)—is less often found than autumnal hawkbit (*L. autumnalis*) and is in fact absent from

Hawkbit

Goat's beard

most of Scotland. The best way to identify the rough hawkbit is by the forked hairs which cover the toothed leaves—and you will most likely find the plant on chalk and limestone.

This, again, is a plant whose leaves can add to a salad if you are short of better things!

Penny-cress

This is a rather uncommon plant of fields and waste places, although sometimes a nuisance in the garden. The tiny white flowers are followed by distinctive winged

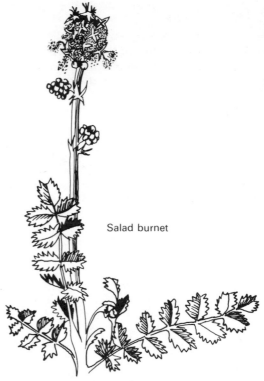

Salad burnet

Penny-cress

seed pods with a deep notch at the top—and which smell unpleasantly when crushed.

The leaves of penny-cress (Latin name *Thlaspi arvense*) have the spicy flavour of watercress.

Salad burnet

Have you ever noticed a cucumber-like smell whilst out walking on chalk grassland on a fine summer day? It comes from the leaves of salad burnet as you crush them underfoot.

So called because it can be used in salads, the salad burnet (*Poterium sanguisorba*) bears balls of greenish-brown flowers on stems less than 0.3 m (1 ft.)

high (called red knobs in Nottinghamshire). In each ball the flowers at the top are female; those in the middle are hermaphrodite (i.e. having the characteristics of both sexes); and those at the bottom are male. Another unusual feature of these flowers is that as they have no nectar to attract insects, the pollen is carried by the wind. The plant is rare in Scotland and Ireland.

The first part of its Latin name comes from a Greek word meaning drinking cup—an allusion to the ancient practice of flavouring wine with this wild plant. Gerard said that this burnet, used in salads for cucumber flavour, 'is thought to make the hart merry and glad, as also being put in wine, to which it yealdeth a certaine grace in the drinking'.

Besides eating salad burnet leaves, slightly braised, in salads, you will also find them pleasant used as the base of a cool, summer drink.

Scurvy grass

So called because the smooth, fleshy leaves contain ascorbic acid (vitamin C), and sailors suffering from scurvy sores were cured by eating the dried herbs or by drinking the juice from this plant.

It is fairly common in salt marshes and on sea-shores around the country except in South-East England. A local name in Yorkshire is scrooby grass. Strangely enough, an alpine form of scurvy grass is found inland in the North and West—but only at high altitudes.

Scurvy grass

Scurvy grass (*Cochlearia officinalis*) has shiny round leaves and white flowers followed by semi-transparent small seed pods.

To eat: There is a choice here—the bitter-tasting leaves, with their high concentration of vitamin C, are beneficial eaten raw; they can be eaten in dried form; or used in drinks.

Watercress

Like the scurvy grass just mentioned, this familiar old English salad is also rich in vitamin C and used to be prescribed for the treatment of scurvy. It is a native British plant, common everywhere in streams and around springs—especially if the water is rich in lime.

The plant (Latin, *Nasturtium officinale*) varies in height between only 150 mm (6 in.) and 0.6 m (2 ft.) and its leaves remain green all the year round. Another common watercress (*N. microphyllum*) has leaves which turn brown in autumn.

To eat: First, a warning—never put watercress in the refrigerator since the texture is then lost. A shallow bowl of water in a cool place is ideal.

To make an excellent watercress salad dice some waxy new potatoes and drop them into a little salted cream. Cover the bottom of a flat dish with sliced tomatoes, and over this shred a little parsley. On this green bed place a layer of the potatoes and finally cover it all with watercress sprigs. Serve dry and do not spoil the flavour with pepper.

Mrs Beeton, in her 1861 *Book of Household Management*, has a splendid hint for a watercress garnish with poultry:

Wash and dry the watercress, pick them nicely and arrange them in a flat layer on a dish. Sprinkle over them a little salt and three tablespoons of vinegar. Place over these the fowl and pour over it the gravy.

A favourite of mine is watercress soup. This charming dish is a revelation to those who do not realise that watercress can be cooked. And here is how to prepare it:

Cook a pound of floury potatoes in salted water until they are three parts done, then add a good bunch of watercress, well washed and chopped up, and cook on until the potatoes are tender enough to pass through a sieve.

Rub the drained potatoes and cress

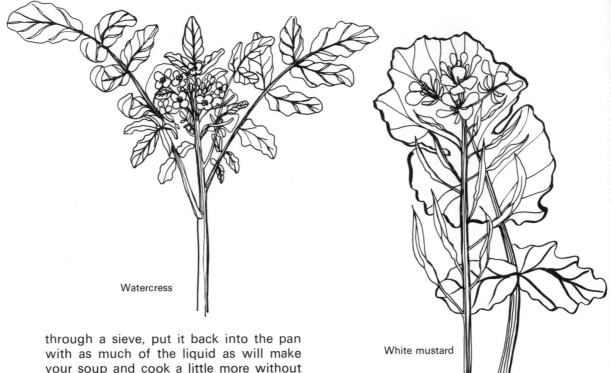

Watercress

White mustard

through a sieve, put it back into the pan with as much of the liquid as will make your soup and cook a little more without letting it boil. Season with pepper and salt and bind with a few spoonsful of cream off the milk.

You can garnish it with a few chopped watercress leaves—but remember to use water, not stock, as (despite what many cook books say) the stock will ruin the splendid fresh flavour of the watercress.

Dr Nicholas Culpeper, in his *Compleat Herbal* of 1653, declared: 'Watercress pottage is a good remedy to cleanse the blood in the spring, and help headaches, and consume the gross humours winter has left behind; those that would live in health, may use it if they please; if they will not, I cannot help it. If any fancy not pottage, they may eat the herb as sallad.'

White mustard

This plant has spread from cultivated areas to persist as a weed on arable land, especially on lime-rich soils in eastern England. It grows up to 0.9 m (3 ft.) tall

and, like the cultivated black mustard, has yellow four-petalled flowers. Mustard is, of course, best known as a condiment (prepared from the seeds) and salad plant, but it is also grown as a fodder crop and to enrich the soil when ploughed in as a green manure.

White mustard (its Latin name is *Sinapis alba*) is quite useful as a salad ingredient, but pick the leaves when young.

Winter cress

Although once valued as a salad, this common plant of stream banks and wet places generally disappeared from the table when better flavoured cultivated plants arrived— but it is still a useful edible and free-for-the-picking wild plant (Latin, *Barbarea vulgaris*). The leaves can also be cooked as a green vegetable.

It is a tall plant, growing to over 0.9 m (3 ft.) and has dark divided leaves each with a

Winter cress

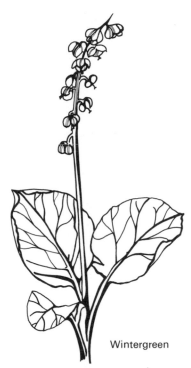

Wintergreen

large round terminal lobe. In May yellow, wallflower-like blooms appear.

Wintergreen

There are about five varieties of this plant, some of them rare, but the edible type (*Pyrola minor*) can be found in the north of England and Scotland, on the moors and in pine woods where—in winter and when most plants have died away—its leaves remain evergreen. These leaves are large and round, resembling those of a pear tree, and indeed the scientific name comes from the Latin word for pear.

As I have said earlier in this section, the leaves of wintergreen can be used in a salad (quite popular in America) or as a substitute for tea. The plant's red berries make a good pie filling.

July

Two trees, as distinct from wild plants, are included in this book since their leaves are

a source of free food. The beech has already been included in an earlier section; this month in the alphabetical descriptions of salad leaves, comes the lime whose flowers as well as leaves have some delicious uses (see pages 36–7). First in the July list, however, comes:

Corn sow thistle

This is a tall perennial with yellow, thistle-like leaves which exude a milky white juice when the stems are broken (the plant is sometimes called field milk-thistle). There are three or four types of sow thistle but the most edible one is *Sonchus arvensis* and is common in corn fields, on marshes and on wasteland throughout the low-lands.

The name sow thistle was thought by William Coles in the seventeenth century to derive from 'a certain natural instinct' in sows whereby they knew it would increase the flow of their milk when they had far-rowed.

Corn sow thistle

To eat corn sow thistle in salad you must first trim off the bristles from the edges of young leaves.

Local names: Milk thistle, in the Midlands; milkweed, milky dashel and milky dickle in Devon and Somerset; sow bread, Kent; and sow dingle, Lincolnshire.

Greater prickly lettuce

This (*Lactuca virosa*) is the stouter of two varieties of prickly lettuce, the other being *L. serriola*, and both are fairly rare. When one does find greater prickly lettuce it is usually on sand dunes by the sea in South and East England.

The plant grows up to 1.8 m (6 ft.) tall and has pale yellow flowers, open in the mornings only, and saw-edged dark green leaves, with fruit coloured dark maroon or nearly black. Prickly lettuce is called a 'compass plant' since, when fully in the sun its leaves always lie in a north–south plane. Some botanists think it may have been introduced from eastern Europe for

its medicinal value—the drug lactucarium, made from the milky juice which (as with sow thistle) seeps from the broken stems and leaves, was a popular sleep-inducer in the Middle Ages.

Greater prickly lettuce

To eat: The flavour of greater prickly lettuce is bitter and very different from the related garden lettuce. Nevertheless, it is a salad ingredient.

Lime

With the soft new leaves of this stately tree (the lime commonly seen is a hybrid between two rare native wild limes, the broad-leaved lime and the small-leaved) one can make a delicately flavoured sandwich filling.

Gather with scissors, while the shell-pink scale leaves still cling to the opened leaf buds. Cut off the stalks and rinse under running water. Then you can either use white bread and butter spread with the lime leaves and sprinkled with lemon juice; or brown bread and butter, cream cheese and lime leaves. Yet another way to enjoy

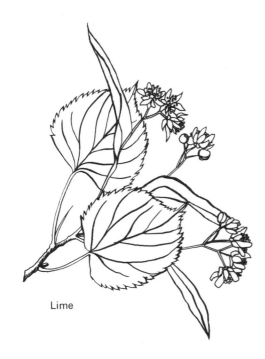

Lime

good to heale the ulcers of the nipples of women's breasts'. The seventeenth-century English botanist and gardener John Parkinson translated papillaris into the English nipplewort.

The flowering plant is easy to identify. Its small heads of about twenty yellow flowers, borne on stems up to 0.9 m (3 ft.) high, open early in the morning and close again early in the afternoon—on a dull day they remain shut.

Nipplewort

this free food is to shred up the leaves and sprinkle with pepper and salt, together with a moistening of cream—eat with white bread.

The flowers of lime, gathered in July and lightly dried, make a very good, pale 'China' tea—both fragrant and refreshing. Use a small handful of dried lime blossom to a medium-sized pot, and infuse with boiling water. Lime tea can be used to induce sweat in fevers.

Nipplewort

Except in mountainous districts this plant (*Lapsana communis*) grows by roadsides, in woodlands, on walls and waste places all over Britain.

It is so-named simply because the buds resemble a woman's nipples—it was once use as a cure for sore nipples (a good case of sympathetic magic!). The plant was called *Papillaris* by German apothecaries because—according to the sixteenth-century writer, Joachim Camerarius—'it is

To eat: The leaves of nipplewort make a useful salad ingredient.
Local names: Carpenter's apron, Warwickshire; hasty rogers or hasty sargeant, West Country; Mary alone, Gloucestershire.

Sea purslane

With minute green flowers, this is a common plant around the coasts of England and Wales.

Halimione (part of its Latin name

Sea purslane

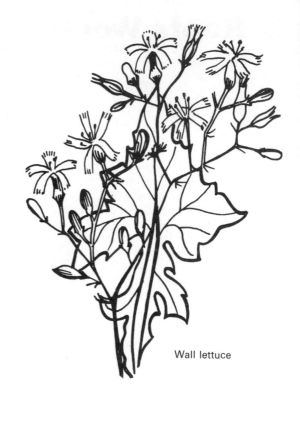

Wall lettuce

Halimione portulacoides) is Greek for 'daughter of the sea'—for this salt-marsh species is covered by most high tides. It is a much-branched plant about 0.6 m (2 ft.) high and—except in the North—abundant, especially along the edges of muddy creeks. The entire plant, covered in a grey-coloured 'flour' formed by bladder-like hairs, bears male and female flowers on the same plant.

The oval, fleshy leaves are a succulent addition to salads, but should be used only for this purpose.

Wall lettuce

This is so named because it occurs frequently on walls, rocks and in shady beechwoods. It is common, except in East Anglia, Devon and Cornwall, Scotland and Ireland.

It is another plant, like sow thistle and the greater prickly lettuce, which has milky juice. Wall lettuce (*Lactura muralis*) grows up to about 0.6 m (2 ft.) high, with yellow flowers.

Use as a salad ingredient.

3. Roots Worth Eating

At almost any time of the year there are getting on for a score of different wild plant roots worth gathering to eat, and the plants described below do not include edible roots of very rare and protected plants—such as the early purple orchis—for obvious conservation reasons.

Despite this precaution, I would however again stress the need to consider others—wild life as well as humans—and harvest only what you need in reasonable quantities, without greed and without damage to, or disfigurement of, the rural environment.

There is no point in a seasonal grouping of roots, as given for leaves, but the plants continue to be arranged alphabetically for easy reference.

Bitter vetch

All five common species of vetch (Latin, *Vicia*) are scrambling plants with pea-like flowers. Vetchling, of which there are ten British species (scientific name *Lathyrus*), differs from vetch in having leaves with only one or two leaflets, instead of several pairs, or even in having no leaves at all.

The perennial vetch we are concerned with is *L. montanus*, sometimes called tuberous pea. It is found on moors and heathlands, and woods in hilly country especially in the North and West. This vetch grows only up to 0.3 m (1 ft.) high and is without tendrils.

The plant has a creeping rhizome, swollen in places to form tubers, and it is these roots which are peeled and chopped to make a boiled vegetable. In the Western Isles of Scotland bitter vetch roots are

Bitter vetch

eaten fresh and raw; they are also used for flavouring whisky.

Thus Gerard on the roots of bitter vetch, which he likened to chestnuts:

they nourish no lesse than the Parsneps: they are not so windie as they, they do more slowly passe throwe the belly by reason of their binding qualitie, and being eaten rawe, they be yet harder of digestion, and do hardlier and slowlier descend.

Local names: Nipper nuts, Somerset; peasling, Yorkshire; caperoiles, Scotland; corra-meile, Hebrides; and fairy's corn, Ireland.

Dittander

Not a common plant but it can be found in salt marshes along the coast—its tall blue-green leaves are long and smooth, its flowers white. At one time dittander was grown in gardens and used as a sauce—it tastes hot and bitter—before pepper and horse-radish replaced it. (Latin name, *Lepidium latifolium*.) Its alternative name of pepperwort indicates its chief use.

Dittander

Flowering rush

A water plant usually found only in central and southern England, this is not really a rush at all. The plant, with handsome soft pink flowers and bold red stamens, is on show from July to September in slow-running streams and canals. It was probably called flowering rush because of its long, narrow rush-like leaves which rise above the surface of the water. Its Latin name is *Butomus umbellatus*.

Flowering rush

In parts of the South and West flowering rush is sometimes called pride of the Thames, and it was first recorded from the river Thames. In the United States this beautiful plant has been introduced to gardens.

Use the root of flowering rush, peeled and chopped, as a cooked vegetable—but go carefully, it is such a beautiful water plant.

Herb bennet

Wood avens is a familiar alternative name for this plant—found not only in woods but in damp places everywhere. It has a small yellow flower like a miniature geum (and the plant is, in fact, a member of that flower family, with the Latin name *Geum urbanum*), and reddish fruit heads with tiny 'hooks' which help distribute the seed by catching on passing animals or birds.

In the sixteenth century herb bennet was grown as a pot herb for use in broth, or sometimes it was drunk as a cure for an upset stomach. Gerard said, 'the rootes taken up in Autumne and dried, do keep

Herb bennet

The plant's roots were once favoured as a relief for stomach upsets, and one reason why it is so often found growing around old coaching inns is because the pungent

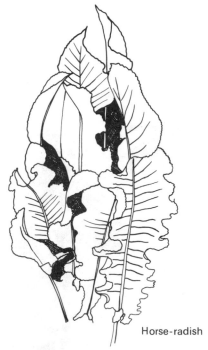

Horse-radish

garments from being eaten with Mothes, and make them to have an excellent good odour'.

The roots of herb bennet do, in fact, have a sweet, clove-like smell and can be used, chopped and in small quantities, to flavour soups and stews.

Horse-radish

First introduced into this country from the Middle East in the fifteenth century as an alternative to mustard, horse-radish—a tough and hardy plant—has now become naturalised on wasteland, in fields and beside streams all over Britain—except Ireland, where it is rare.

The spreading of horse-radish (*Armoracia rusticana*) is almost entirely by the roots or underground stems as the seed rarely sets in the British climate.

Horse-radish can be identified by its large, wavy dock-like leaves alone; the lower ones are often deeply divided like the teeth of a comb whilst the upper leaves are small and undivided.

juice extracted from its roots formed a hot cordial for cold or sick men and horses.

Horse-radish made into strong fomentations can be useful to relieve a cold or neuralgia, and it has its medicinal use as an embrocation—for this one uses the juice mixed with the yolk of an egg.

It may make you weep when peeling and grating horse-radish roots but the ivory shreds make a fine cold sauce, inseparable from beef, and quite outstanding when eaten with smoked trout and brown bread and butter. For this, mix the scraped horse-radish with whipped cream, add a little salt and chill before serving.

Hot horse-radish sauce (very good with fish and with boiled beef and carrots) is prepared by making a cream sauce with flour, butter and milk. When this has boiled well, stir in finely grated horse-radish root; let this remain just long enough to heat through before stirring in a lump of butter and enough mustard to make a pleasant cream colour. Serve piping hot. This is best with an oily kind of fish such as mackerel.

Large evening primrose

Introduced as a garden flower from North America, this fragrant yellow-flowered plant has spread widely in England, Wales and southern Scotland, especially on sand dunes. It grows 0.6 to 0.9 m (2 to 3 ft.) tall and the flowers, opening on summer evenings, are pollinated by night-flying moths.

More closely related to willowherb than to the primrose family, the roots of *Oenothera biennis* (as the plant is known botanically) can be boiled as a vegetable—and so can the young shoots.

Lords and ladies

Although the roots of this familiar and strange plant, more correctly called cuckoo-pint, have their practical uses, it is one to treat with caution as its bright red berries which appear inside a pale green sheath in July and August are poisonous—fatally so to children.

The plant is scientifically called *Arum maculatum* (hence, presumably, why as a boy in the Midlands, I called them arum lilies) and in the hedgerows in April appears the cowl-like green and purple sheath surrounding a stem bearing separate male and female flowers. The colours, and the flower's odd stench, attract small flies which are trapped in the sheath by downward-pointing hairs until they have carried out pollination; only when the delicate sheath withers do they—well covered with pollen—escape to visit another flower.

However, despite its spike of dangerous red berries, the baked roots of cuckoo-pint are a useful substitute for arrowroot as a thickening agent for sauces, soups and stews. In the Middle Ages a white starch was made from cuckoo-pint roots.

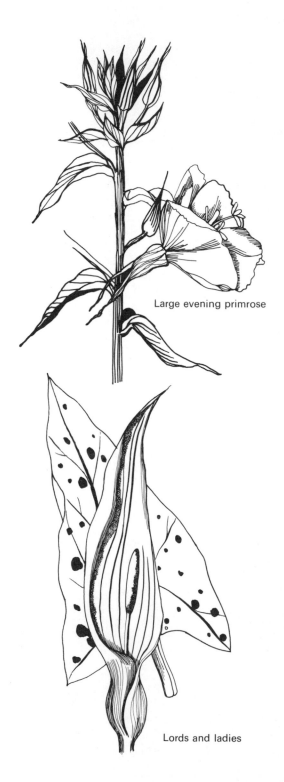

Large evening primrose

Lords and ladies

Few British wild plants, edible or otherwise, have a greater folklore attached to them—or more peculiar local name variations—than the cuckoo-pint. There is no one better to quote on this than Geoffrey Grigson in his *Englishman's Flora*:

The mediaeval 'Agnus Castus, A Middle English Herbal', calls Arum maculatum cokkowyl pyntyl, *which at first sight looks like cuckold's pintle. There seems some folk-etymological confusion between cuckoo, cuckold and cuculle = hood, cowl, Latin* cucullus, *in the name Cuckoopint . . . The robin of the name Wake Robin [there are, for cuckoo-pint, names equivalent to this in German, French, Dutch, Swedish and Danish!] may also be explained as 'penis on the alert', a use of Robin as a pet name for the penis.*

Local names: As I have said, the flower spike bears separate male and female flowers and this gives rise to many of the local names being male plus female—like Adam and Eve or bulls and cows, used in the east Midlands and Yorkshire. Other picturesque names include—angels and devils, Somerset; Bobbin and Joan, Northants; devils, ladies and gentlemen, North Wales; knights and ladies, Somerset; lords and ladies, a name used all over the country and with the variation lords' and ladies' fingers, in Warwickshire; parson-in-the-pulpit, Yorkshire and parts of the West Country; and—oddest of all perhaps—when I was working in the Weald of Kent I was told the plant was there called Kitty-come-down-the-lane-jump-up-and-kiss-me.

Marsh mallow

This is becoming rare, as more marshes are drained for agricultural and other uses. The plant is taller than the common mallow (*Malva sylvestris*) which has pink, single flowers and is frequently seen by roadsides. The marsh mallow is a different species (botanically called *Althaea officinalis*—our garden hollyhocks belong to the Althaea family) although its flowers are also pink—and its leaves and stems are down-covered.

Marsh mallow, as the name implies, is chiefly found on salt marshes and beside ditches near the sea in the South.

As it was believed that the sweets cured a wide range of diseases, marsh mallow

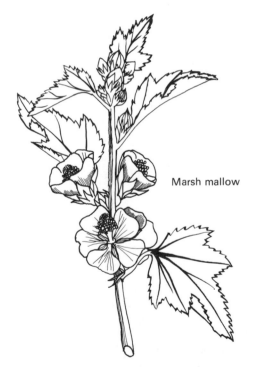

Marsh mallow

confectionery was once made in the London area from the dried, powdered roots of this plant. I confess that, although I have included marsh mallow among accepted edible roots, I can find no recipe for making the sweets or doing much else

43

with these roots—but some country folk have it in their herb gardens.

Restharrow

This is, although growing less than 0.6 m (2 ft.) high, a handsome and jaunty wild plant with pink flowers, and one which delighted us as children; in parts of the Midlands and the North Country, we dug up the roots to chew—tough as they were —as 'wild liquorice' Correctly speaking, wild liquorice is another plant altogether, with the tortuous Latin name *Astragalus glycyphyllos*, a relative of which is the source of commercial liquorice.

I said the roots of restharrow (*Ononis repens*) are tough—so much so, in fact, that they delayed the passage of horse ploughs or harrows and this is how the plant got its name. It is common on chalky grassland.

If you crush the leaves of restharrow between your fingers they give off an unpleasant, goat-like smell, and if cattle

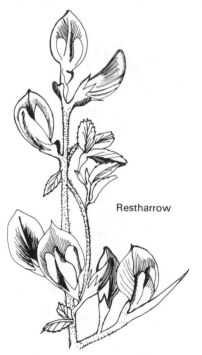

Restharrow

eat the leaves their milk becomes tainted with this same smell—particularly if the milk is made into cheese, which is then said to be 'cammocky'. Hence the reason why it is said that the proper English name for restharrow is cammock.

Spiny restharrow (*Ononis spinosa*) is a similar plant of clay soils in the South and East, but lacks underground stems. The West Coast has yet another variety, called small restharrow (*O. reclinata*).

Local names: These reflect the main use for the roots of this plant—to chew as liquorice or, as liquorice was then called in the North, Spanish Juice: thus we get Spanish root, in Cumberland; wild liquorice in Yorkshire and elsewhere; hen-goose, west Midlands; stayplough, Somerset; and stinking tam, in Northumberland.

Salsify

This is a similar species to goat's beard already described on p. 31, but has purple flowers. It is usually found as an escapee from gardens, especially near the sea (Latin name, *Tragopogon porrifolius*).

Salsify is a good-looking plant in the wild or in the garden, with its tall, pinkish-purple flowers. The root has a curiously salt, fishy flavour (it is sometimes called the vegetable oyster). As Dorothy Hartley puts it: 'It is certainly a vegetable to eat by itself, and so like oyster that it takes in the cat.'

To eat: Lift and scrape salsify roots with care. Tie together in bundles, boil or steam and then cut them loose and fry to an appetising brown. Another idea is to egg-and-breadcrumb the roots before frying and serve with slices of lemon, like fillets of fish.

For delicious baked salsify the method is to boil the roots until soft, then when they are cool enough, scrape and rub off their outer skin. Slice the long, fishy, grey-coloured and translucent root into oval cuts—laying them in a buttered pie dish. Dredge with crumbs, just moisten with the

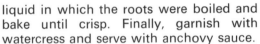

Salsify

Sea holly

liquid in which the roots were boiled and bake until crisp. Finally, garnish with watercress and serve with anchovy sauce.

Sea holly

Once common on sand and shingle everywhere around the coast, this plant is now rare in the North and East and becoming so elsewhere as a result of human invasion. It has waxy, prickly leaves and a pale blue, thistle-like flower.

Roots of sea holly (Latin, *Eryngium maritimum*) penetrate five or six feet through the sand. Candied roots were formerly considered good for those 'that have no delight or appetite to venery' and 'nourishing and restoring the aged'. The roots of sea holly, known as eringoes, were candied with sugar and orange flower-water and sold as late as Victorian times.

Today, sea holly roots are best used as a vegetable—peeled and boiled until soft.

Silverweed

A plant, widespread in damp grassy and waste places, with yellow flowers and

Silverweed

45

much-divided silvery leaves (this silvery effect is produced by long, silky hairs).

Silverweed is thought to have got its Latin name (*Potentilla anserina*) because it grows freely on grassland where geese feed, the 'anser', part of its botanical name, meaning a goose.

The plant spreads by creeping rooted stems and once had many uses, including treatment for ulcers and sores; it was also placed in boots to keep long-distance walkers' feet comfortable.

Before the introduction of the potato, silverweed was extensively grown in west Scotland and its roots boiled, dried and ground into flour for bread or porridge. This is exactly the use to which we can put the plant nowadays.

Star of Bethlehem

This is so called because the plant has white star-like flowers and is abundant in Palestine. Botanists are not sure whether this is a native wild flower or one, like the large evening primrose described on page 42 which has escaped from gardens—it may be genuinely only a native of sandy grassland in the Breckland of East Anglia.

Each white petal of Star of Bethlehem (Latin name, *Ornithogalum umbellatum*) has a green stripe on the back which can only be clearly seen before the flower opens in the middle of the morning—the reason why a popular name for the plant is 'ten o'clock lady'.

Although the plant is poisonous to cattle, we can eat the bulbous root. Just peel the bulbs and use as a boiled vegetable.

Local names: Betty-go-to-bed-at-noon, Shropshire; starry eyes, Somerset; six o'clock flower, Midlands; and shamefaced maiden, Wiltshire.

Turnip

The wild variety of this staple farm root crop is botanically known as *Brassica rapa*.

Star of Bethlehem

Turnip

It is familiar throughout the British Isles and useful as either a green vegetable (for which you should pick the tender young leaves) or as a root vegetable, boiled or roasted.

White waterlily

Go easy with this beautiful plant, even though it can be found in very many ponds and lakes and its underwater tubers are pleasant when boiled tender in salted water.

The white variety (*Nymphaea alba*) is less common than the yellow waterlily (*Nuphar lutea*).

The rooting stems of the white waterlily were at one time used as a cure for baldness. An interesting feature of the plant is the fruit capsule which ripens under water, then splits to release the seeds—and these have air in their seedcoats enabling them to float.

Wild parsnip

White waterlily

Wild parsnip

This is often found on chalk hills in the South and on wasteland generally; the Latin name is *Pastinaca sativa*. Although the roots are not as large as the garden type of parsnip they are worth trying. Dig up the parsnip roots, preferably after early frosts, peel and quarter them. The parsnip pieces are boiled in water until soft then rubbed through a sieve. Roasting is an alternative, and for this it is wise first to remove the tough central core.

Did you know that parsnips also make good 'chips'? For these, scrape the parsnips and cut into four quarters, top to tail; these pieces must next be sliced to about the thickness of a pencil. Put your chips into cold water and boil for a few minutes, drain off the water and dry. Now the chips are ready to dip in dry flour and fry just as you would do potato chips.

There are few better country open-air suppers than a hot dish of crisp parsnip chips served with baked tomatoes and hot dripping toast!

4. Stems for Cooking

Not many wild plants have edible stems suitable for cooking compared with the wide range of leaves and roots we can use, but they do include some outstanding delicacies such as marsh samphire—so renowned in Norfolk—and seakale which is comparable with asparagus.

The stems described below can be gathered any time from the spring through to late autumn, but the younger the better.

Alexanders

This is a somewhat rare plant, found in hedgerows, wasteland and on cliffs near the coastline—growing up to 1.2 m (4 ft.) tall and having yellow flowers. It is a mem-

Alexanders

ber of the parsley family (and introduced here from the Mediterranean by the Romans) all of which are botanically known as *Umbelliferae* because the flowers are arranged, umbrella-like, on ribs that spread from a central stem. There are seventy or so British species.

The solid, furrowed stems of alexanders (Latin, *Smyrnium olusatrum*) taste like boiled celery when cooked young; the toothed leaves of the plant can also be used as a flavouring herb or as spice in salads. These leaves come very early, sometimes even through January snows.

Cut the pinkish part of the leaf stems growing near the base of the alexander plant; there they are thick and partly blanched by surrounding foliage. Cook for up to ten minutes in boiling water—this gets rid of the plant's odd, cloying smell and the result is a very pleasant, aromatic taste when these stems are eaten like asparagus with melted butter.

Local names: Alick, Kent; hellroot, Dorset; megweed, Sussex; skit, Cornwall.

Bracken

This is perhaps the best known of over fifty species of fern in the British Isles—and all ferns (in fossil form, ferns date back 300 million years) are distinguished from other plants by clumps of spores on the undersides of their leaves. Being flowerless, ferns reproduce from these spores instead of seeds.

Bracken (*Pteridium aquilinum*) is basically a woodland species, and on mountains it never grows above the timber line.

Bracken

Young bracken fronds, about 75 mm (3 in.) high, should be snapped off and cooked like asparagus—only longer—and served with melted bacon-fat and brown bread and butter. They have a smoky flavour and you will either like bracken tips very much or not at all!

Burdock

Three species of this herb are common, except in the far north. Great burdock (*Arctium lappa*) is the familiar big roadside plant with leaves like rhubarb, solid stalks and clinging, bur-covered seedheads; then there is a much smaller burdock (*A. minus*) with hollow leaf stalks; and wood burdock (*A. vulgare*). The stalks and roots of all three are edible—they are used in medicines for skin diseases as well as having kitchen uses.

To eat: Cut the young stems into short lengths, peel off the thick outer skin and chop up for a salad ingredient—it has a crisp, nutty flavour. Or you can boil until

tender and add to meat soups. The stalks of the flowers can also be used.

Burdock stalks and roots used to be boiled or eaten raw as a tonic and an aphrodisiac—Gerard spoke of its use 'to increase seed and stir up lust'. An essence made from the plant is used in the preparation of dandelion and burdock, the equivalent of today's 'coke' when I was a child.

Lesser Burdock

Local names: Because of its rhubarb-like leaves it is in many parts of the country called gipsy's rhubarb, pig's rhubarb, wild rhubarb and similar. Some other descriptive names are gipsy's comb, Nottinghamshire; hurr-burr, Leicestershire; sticky buds, Wiltshire; touch-me-not, or turkey rhubarb, Somerset; and tuzzy-muzzy, in Devon.

Celery

This is closely related to the cultivated plant and is another member of the umbrella-flowered parsley family (Latin, *Apium graveolens*).

Celery

countryside. It has handsome, bright yellow flower clusters, although the first part of its Latin name *Silybum marianum* means thistle-like. It is only locally common, often near the sea.

Milk thistle grows up to 1.8 m (6 ft.) tall, with spiny leaves veined in white. Almost all parts of the milk thistle are edible, but the best-known use is to peel the stems and stew like rhubarb. But first soak them well in water to remove the bitterness. (See also corn sow thistle, p. 35.)

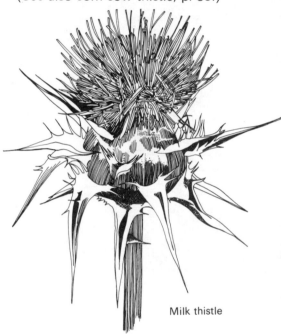

Milk thistle

Also like alexanders, wild celery has a furrowed stem and a strong smell—maybe this is why some writers have quite wrongly described the plant as poisonous. It certainly is not, and wild celery was widely used in medieval kitchens as a dried herb; and, as chopped stems, it is said to be a good ingredient in fresh salads. I have not myself tried it, as I have most of the other plants in this book, but Richard Mabey recommends cream of wild celery as 'much richer and tangier than garden celery soup', and for this he advises drying a small bunch of leaves (in a little-used room!) for about three weeks, then simmering them for about half an hour in some chicken broth. Strain, stir in a cupful of hot milk and serve immediately.

Wild celery is common in damp places, especially near the sea, but mainly in the southern part of the country. Its flowers are white.

Milk thistle

This is not one of the eleven sorts of ordinary, purple-flowered thistles of the

Samphire

Of this succulent and delectable plant there are many species, growing in salt marshes around the coast.

It is hard to tell one variety from another; all have jointed, much-branched stems varying from 25 to 380 mm (1 to 15 in.). The difficulty of identification has led to much confusion between samphire (botanically called *Crithmum maritimum*) and glasswort (*Salicornia stricta*), only added to by the fact that both these shore plants are used to make excellent pickle as well as being a useful cooked vegetable.

Glasswort got its name from the fact that the plant was burnt to produce soda for use in making soap and glass. It is chiefly in eastern England that the plant is called samphire, or marsh samphire.

The true samphire, and its earlier sampere or sampier, comes from the French herbe de St Pierre—herb of the fisherman saint whose name was Petros, or rock. Hence yet another small name variation (rock samphire).

Samphire

To eat: As a vegetable it is best to leave on the little white roots so that, after boiling for ten minutes, you can hold it easily and suck it like asparagus with hot butter poured over it.

To pickle samphire, I quote what John Evelyn in 1706 called 'the Dover receit'.

Let it be gathered about Michaelmas or in the spring and put two or three hours into a brine of water and salt, then into a clean tinned brass pot with three parts of strong white wine vinegar and one part of water and salt or as much as will cover the sampier, keeping the vapour from issuing out by pushing down the pot lid, and so hang it over the fire for half an hour only.

Being taken off let it remain cover'd till it be cold and then put it up into small barrels or jars with the liquor and some fresh vinegar water and salt, and thus it will keep very green.

Finally, on the subject of samphire, a Norfolk innkeeper friend of mine provided an unexpected treat when he handed round the bar some shoots of this plant fresh from the nearby coastline. Chewed raw they were salty and thirst-making!

Seakale

This is an example of indiscriminate and greedy use of a widely available edible wild plant resulting in its becoming scarce on sand, shingle, rocks and cliffs around the coast of Britain. Too many thoughtless people—particularly on the south coast— over-picked it once it was known to be an excellent vegetable when boiled and served with butter. As early as 1731, Philip Miller in his *Gardeners' Dictionary*, remarked that seakale was plentiful on the Sussex coast 'where the inhabitants gather

Seakale

it in the spring to eat, preferring it to any of the cabbage kind'.

The plant (*Crambe maritima*) has blue—green, curly and crisp leaves, grows about 0.6 m (2 ft.) high, and has white, honey-scented flowers from June onwards.

Seakale (spelled seakail in the nineteenth century) had been an English wild plant for hundreds of years, and it is now one of the cultivated vegetables nurserymen have developed from our native flora.

Botanists in the sixteenth century knew it as English kale.

To eat: Strip the leaves from the stems, boil until tender and serve with butter and lemon juice, to be eaten like asparagus. And here is a good tip for seakale with roast duck: boil for ten minutes, drain it; then let it simmer in a rich stock or good brown gravy in which it may be served with the bird.

5. Useful Wild Herbs

Only by trial and error through many centuries has man discovered just which plants are edible and which are poisonous. This is particularly so in the case of herbs, hundreds of which have been used or tried for medicinal and culinary purposes.

A herb is any non-woody flowering plant, more particularly used as a medicine or food. The Romans introduced many herbs to Britain since, like the Greeks, they valued the supposed supernatural qualities of the plants as well as their practical uses. In the Middle Ages the witch used herbs to brew her evil potions and likewise every villager had his herbs to combat her powers—including, for example, herb paris with its poisonous purple berries. The early Christian church used herbs in rites and ceremonies, and herbal remedies were the mainstay of physicians. So, too, the medieval housewife was an expert—indeed far more knowledgeable than we are today—in knowing scores of different edible plants and how best to use them in the kitchen.

Herbs were important in the daily life of the population, in sickness and in health. Wild herbs of value were brought into the garden and these were the antecedents of many of our present-day cultivated vegetables—the wild parsnip, for instance, was until the sixteenth century boiled, baked and even used to sweeten puddings. Similarly, medicinal herbs were also cultivated, often by the monks—and the names given to some plants reflect their ancient medical associations; for instance, what we now call spurge was once wartwort in the Midlands and whitlow-grass in East Anglia since it was used to treat skin diseases. Goutweed (or, correctly, ground elder) is another example of a name indicating medical use.

Today, whilst a wide selection of improved cultivated varieties of vegetables may have replaced many of the wild herbs in the kitchen, there are still a considerable number of wild plants we can and should enjoy as herbs in the culinary sense. And in modern medicine certain drugs are still produced from plants—for example, pain-killing morphine from the dried juice of unripe poppy seed; the heart stimulant digitalis from foxgloves; and atropine (used in the treatment of eye diseases) comes from belladonna, the juice of deadly nightshade.

Below, in seasonal order as well as alphabetically, is a list of just some of the best and safest wild herbs for the modern cook—there are many others not so acceptable to our present-day palate and, in certain cases, herbs not included in my selection can have an irritant effect.

Also omitted for the family's safety are such varieties as the familiar roadside plant called cow parsley because, although it has considerable culinary claims (as well as its hollow, furrowed stems providing children with pea shooters!) there is too much danger of it being confused with several related species—hemlock and fool's parsley in particular—which are poisonous.

April—May

Balm

Beekeepers plant this herb near their hives, as the small white flowers are rich in nectar in August and September when the main nectar-supplying flowers are over—hence the name bee-balm. Formerly grown in gardens for its sweet, lemon-scented flowers, balm (Latin, *Melissa officinalis*) has spread to roadsides in southern England and Ireland.

Balm tea, made by steeping the leaves in boiling water, is sold by herbalists as a 'nerve tonic'.

Lemon balm, as it is often called because of the delicious scent, grows into a big soft bush of lush green leaves not unlike the

Balm

nettle, but less jagged. It was strewn over the rushes on the floors of dwellings in the Middle Ages to give off its refreshing perfume when trodden on.

This is best used fresh, as it does not dry well. It is useful to replace lemon juice and a few leaves are pleasant in a salad, or to give aroma to summer drinks. Also delightful as a garnish for Pimm's Cup.

Borage

There is a faint cucumber flavour to the hairy leaves of this plant (*Borago officinalis*). It has brilliant blue, star-like flowers and can be found on banks and in hedges, mostly in southern England—although originally it was a garden plant.

Gerard, the sixteenth-century herbalist whose fascinating writings I have more than once quoted in this book, wrote of

Borage

borage: 'those of our time do use the flower in salads, to exhilarate and make the minde glad'. A century later John Evelyn declared that sprigs of borage in wine 'are of known virtue to revive the hypochondriac and cheer the hard student'.

As with other herbs listed here, strip the leaves of borage from their stems and use either fresh or dried as flavouring. The blue blossom, together with scarlet nasturtium flowers, makes a beautiful salad garnish.

To use borage sprigs in wine, a Victorian recipe for a claret cup advises using a teaspoonful of white sugar dissolved in boiling water, one glass of sherry, half a glass of brandy, thin rind of lemon, a strip of cucumber rind and a bottle of claret. Let it all stand for an hour and when serving the claret cup put in a sprig of borage to impart aroma—then remove the borage and drink up!

Field poppy

An interesting lot of folklore is attached to this plant. It was once thought that smelling the field, or corn, poppy (*Papaver rhoeas*) brought on headaches, and that staring at them too long made you go blind. Children long believed that poppies must not be picked for fear of a thunderstorm—hence such local names as thundercup, thunderflower and lightnings. In Welsh the poppy is llygad y bwgan, or goblin's eye. Superstitions also persist that

Field poppy

the seeds contain opium; in fact no parts of the field poppy are narcotic (opium comes from the species *Papaver somniferum* cultivated in India).

As the common poppy bursts into scarlet flower, the two sepals covering the bud drop off. Its petals were once used to make a syrup and the seeds yield two types of oil—an edible cooking oil and a coarser type used by artists in mixing paints.

When the seed heads of field poppy are brown the seed can easily be shaken out for use in the kitchen. They go pleasantly with honey as a dressing for fruit; or the seeds can be sprinkled on bread, cakes and biscuits.

Local names: Another plant with a host of local descriptive and picturesque alternatives, including cock's comb, cock-rose and cock's head in the North Country; old woman's petticoat, paradise lily and pepper boxes, in the West Country; thunderball, Warwickshire; and red rags, Dorset.

Ground ivy

Despite the name this plant is neither related to ivy nor does it look anything like ivy. It is a short, creeping plant (Latin, *Glechoma hederacea*) with square stems and heart-shaped leaves in pairs. Its clusters of blue flowers resemble violets.

Ground Ivy

Before the cultivation of hops, ground ivy—then known as alehoof—was used to flavour beer, and in parts of Shropshire as a stuffing for pork. Today its best use is as a fragrant, herbal tea—made with boiling water on the dried leaves.

Parsley piert

The name comes from 'perce-pierre', a Flemish term meaning a plant which pierces its way through strong ground— hence the old herbalists thought it useful in cases of stone in the human bladder!

The plant (*Aphanes arvensis*) is common in fields and dry waste places. The

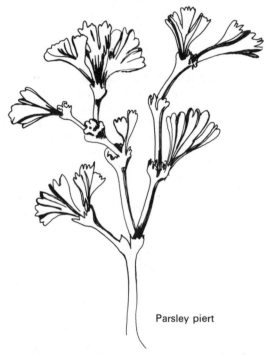

Parsley piert

leaves can be chopped and used as a salad herb. Also, in his *The English Physitian Enlarged* (1669) Nicholas Culpeper recommends parsley piert for pickling.

Ramsons

This is the only British wild plant whose leaf-stalk is twisted through 180 degrees,

Ramsons

and its starry white flowers are often seen with bluebells and red campion in damp woodland.

The plant (*Allium ursinum*) smells like garlic—and it is as a flavouring that one can use the lily-of-the-valley type of leaves. Much of the strong smell disappears on cooking.

Woodruff

Another common plant in moist woods, particularly on chalk soils. Woodruff grows about 0.3 m (1 ft.) high, with smooth, rather squarish stems and small white flowers in loose heads.

The plant smells of new-mown hay when it is crushed. Woodruff (*Asperula odorata*) was formerly used to scent bed linen. As a dried herb it is very pleasant added as a flavouring to cool summer drinks—or you can make a delicious tea from its dried flowers. I have not tried it in wine, but according to Gerard a sprig or two put in wine will 'make a man merrie'.

Woodruff

Chives

Local names: Ladies-in-the-hay, Wiltshire; new-mown-hay, Nottinghamshire; and scented hairwood, or woody-ruffee, in Yorkshire.

June–July

Chives

This is another member of the onion family (*Allium schoenoprasum*). Originally from northern Europe, it now grows wild in Britain—mainly on limestone cliffs near fresh water. There are also several species of wild leeks but these too are rare and very local.

Chives are very acceptable with cream cheese, omelettes and in salads.

Crow garlic

This is the wild onion. When it was common in meadows cattle ate it with the result that milk and butter had an unpleasant flavour. Better cultivation has largely eliminated it from farmland and the plant (*Allium vineale*), which has pink or greenish-white flowers, is now found on roadsides, usually on heavy, clay soils. It can be used, when all else is lacking, as a flavouring—but it is not highly recommended!

Crow garlic

Fennel

Yet another plant of the parsley family, some of which have already been described, and thought to be a naturalised medicinal herb.

Longfellow wrote:

The Fennel, with its yellow flowers,
In an earlier age than ours,
Was gifted with the wondrous
   powers
Lost vision to restore . . .

Fennel (*Foeniculum vulgare*) is a strong-smelling tall plant, with feathery leaves and yellowish flowers. It is not

Fennel

common—but can be found on sea cliffs. Often grown in gardens, its chief use is dried, to flavour sauce for fish—especially mackerel. Or it can be used for fennel-flavoured butter.

Meadowsweet

Just as people in the Middle Ages gave a refreshing odour to their homes with lemon balm strewn over the rushes on the floors so did they use for a similar purpose the familiar scented creamy-white blossoms of meadowsweet, or queen of the meadows.

No one can have any doubt about the identification of the dense clusters of this flower (*Filipendula ulmaria*) which line the banks of roadside ditches and streams right through to September.

Meadowsweet has several medicinal uses, including the treatment of malaria; its name is, however, derived from its use to

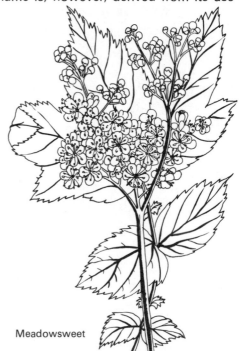

Meadowsweet

flavour the honey-based drink called mead—hence one of its alternative names, meadwort. The dried leaves were also used to give an aromatic bouquet to port and claret.

Today we use either the dried or fresh leaves of meadowsweet as a flavouring herb.

Its local names are almost all variations on the word meadow—except for an odd Cumberland name, courtship and matrimony, which refers to the difference in scent before and after crushing the plant!

Mints

There are several wild mints—among them corn mint (*Mentha arvensis*), which is common in fields but lacks a minty smell, and water mint (*Mentha aquatica*) with showy pink flowers and a strong scent. Both are common everywhere.

Peppermint (*M. piperita*), one of the important commercial hybrid varieties of mint, can very occasionally also be found growing wild. Spear-mint (*M. spicata*), the common garden mint, is widespread as a wild plant in very localised areas.

Calamint   Water mint

All the mints are, of course, used fresh or dried as flavouring—including common calamint (*Calamintha ascendens*), occasionally found on chalky soil hedge-banks.

Sweet cicely

This old pot-herb with sweet-scented leaves is wild in the North Country and often to be found along mountain roads in Scotland. It grows up to 1.5 m (5 ft.) tall, and according to Culpeper, the candied roots of this plant (*Myrrhis odorata*) were able to prevent infection by the plague.

Sweet cicely—the name refers as much to taste as to smell—has a number of uses: a wood polish can be made from its leaves;

Sweet cicely

it is used as a herb in the making of the liqueur, Chartreuse; and its feathery leaves make a mild aniseed-like flavouring for stewed fruit.

Wild thyme

Once thought to be a cure for headaches, this attractive little plant—a favourite with bees—forms a dense carpet of reddish-purple flowers on dry grassland and heaths.

Use wild thyme (*Thymus drucei*) in any recipe in which you would normally include the cultivated variety.

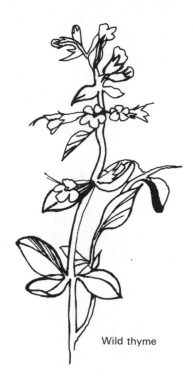

Wild thyme

July–September

Lady's bedstraw

This sprawling, feathery little yellow-flowered plant is common in grassy places almost everywhere and several quaint legends are attached to it. In the evening or when the air is damp, the flowers of lady's bedstraw (Latin name, *Galium verum*) give off a scent of honey, and the plant dries with the smell of hay—pleasant attributes which probably in olden days encouraged the plant's use as a soft base on which to sleep, particularly because such bedding could easily be burnt and a fresh supply brought in.

Legend has it that it was lady's bedstraw upon which the Virgin lay during the Nativity. In some remote parts of Germany women put lady's bedstraw in their beds to make childbirth easier and safer—an attribute also credited to the herb called penny-royal (*Mentha pulegium*), an uncommon

plant of damp heathland in the West and a veritable herbalist's cure-all!

The plant has several other interesting uses—physicians, for instance, used it as a blood coagulant and it had long been

Lady's bedstraw

widely used both to extract red dye from its stems, and to curdle milk for cheese and junket making. In 1664 Robert Turner wrote that 'the decotion of the herb and flowers used warm, is excellent good to bathe the surbated Feet of Footmen and Lackies in hot weather'.

Currently, the leaves of lady's bedstraw are most commonly used as flavouring.

Local names: From reasons given above, Warwickshire folk call the plant cheese rennet; in Suffolk it is fleaweed (doubtless referring to its astringent uses in bed); and a Manx name is 'lus-y-volley' meaning herb of the sweet smell.

Marjoram

The variety usually used as a pungent herb in the kitchen is a Mediterranean species

Marjoram

(*Origanum onites*) but we have a useful aromatic wild variety (*O. vulgare*) common in lime-rich grassland except in the North and Scotland.

It is easily identified by its rose-purple flowers, at the top of a 0.6 m (2 ft.) stem, in oblong spikes similar to those of mint.

Marjoram is a most provident plant. It contains an oil sold in shops as oil of thyme, once used as a pain killer; the flowering tops yield a purple dye for wool; and the small, downy leaves make a herb tea. Because it is one of our most aromatic herbs, marjoram is excellent as stuffing for poultry, or for flavouring soups, stews and sauces.

Tansy

This was formerly much valued in the kitchen as a flavouring, and in some areas tansy pudding was eaten at Easter in remembrance of the 'bitter herbe' eaten by the Jews at the Passover.

It is a tall herb with fern-like leaves and a flat-topped golden-yellow flower head (Latin name, *Chrysanthemum vulgare*). It can be found everywhere, and has a spicy, lemon scent and bitter flavour.

Tansy is so useful that it was once brought into cottage gardens for cooking,

Tansy

medicinal purposes (e.g. to staunch wounds and to prevent miscarriages) and as an insect repellent.

Strip off tansy leaves and try them fresh or dried as flavouring. Richard Mabey suggests a delightful-sounding medieval bubble-and-squeak made from a fry-up of tansy leaves, green corn and violets, served with orange and sugar.

The legends surrounding tansy credit it, like lady's bedstraw and pennyroyal, with such amazing surgical benefits as stopping a uterus bleeding and curing the inflammation of a kidney. Culpeper's famous seventeenth-century physician's book declared of tansy: 'Let those Women that desire Children love this Herb, 'tis their best Companion, their Husband excepted.' He advised tansy either bruised and laid bare on the navel, or boiled in beer and drunk to stay miscarriages. On the other hand, girls have been known to try the poisonous oil of tansy to procure abortion.

Wild angelica

This 1.5 m (5 ft.) tall hollow-stemmed plant of damp woods and grass is a member of the parsley family and botanically called *Angelica sylvestris.* Its flowers are white or pinkish, and the plant is related to the angelica whose stems are crystallised and used in confectionary.

Wild angelica

The chopped leaves are good with rhubarb and other stewed fruit.

Be very careful to identify this plant correctly and not to cut poisonous hemlock

by mistake (see my warnings about this on page 16, under Hogweed). Angelica has downy, pink and purple stems; broad, toothed leaves; and large flower heads which some say 'look as if they had been dipped in claret'.

Wild basil

A common purple flowered and hairy perennial found in hedges and by roadsides everywhere in the South, but less often seen in the North. The leaves of wild basil (*Clinopodium vulgare*) can be used in the same manner as the shop herb—excellent for bringing out the flavour of a tomato salad. Basil sherry, made by steeping the fresh leaves in the wine for a couple of weeks, was at one time sprinkled in soups.

Basil-thyme is a different plant (*Acinos arvensis*), common on bare ground in chalk regions of the South and East but rare elsewhere. The plant is aromatic, and herbalist Gerard thought that its 'seede cureth thee infirmities of the hart, taketh away sorrowfulnesse which cometh of melancholic, and maketh a man merrie and glad'.

Wormwood

Called wormit in the North, from its use as an insecticide against fleas, it is an aromatic, exceedingly bitter herb with silvery leaves and yellow flowers. The latter part of its botanical name (*Artemisia absinthium*) is derived from the herb's use, when infused with alcohol, to make the potent French liqueur, absinthe.

Used in small quantities as a flavouring this herb is quite acceptable and claimed to have tonic qualities—it also contains a worm-dispeller, santonin (an overdose of which is dangerous).

The most interesting use for wormwood I have come across is as a constituent of a herb salve for sores and bruises. A Nottinghamshire farmer's wife gave me the following recipe for making the salve and I find it has remarkable healing properties:

Take a handful each of fresh wormwood leaves, elderflowers and groundsel—all cut into 25 mm (1 in.) lengths. Put them into an earthenware pot with a pound of good quality lard and bring to the boil in the oven. Simmer for half an hour, then strain into small jars and tie down when cool.

Wild basil

Wormwood

6. Seaweeds to Enjoy

There are about eight hundred species of seaweeds in Britain and, although not often realised, they have a season of growth just as with other plants. Seaweeds shoot as buds, grow lustily during the summer and wither in the winter. Most of them are rich in health-giving mineral salts and, once you get used to the iodine flavour, they are a fine source of free food.

Before cooking, always wash seaweeds in fresh water—or leave them out in the rain. (If all the salt is not removed the dried seaweed will pick up the damp.)

Carragheen

Of all the common seaweeds, perhaps this has the most culinary uses. Also called Irish moss (botanically called *Chondrus crispus*), it is light purplish-brown—colour is important in identifying seaweeds—and has flat, fan-shaped stalks. Gather in April or May for use either fresh, as a 'blanc-mange' (a Yorkshire treatment) or dried for later use.

To make Irish moss blancmange, add one cup of moss to three cups of milk, add sugar and flavouring (ginger is fine) to taste. Simmer the seaweed in the milk until most of the weed is melted—then strain and pour into a mould to set. By using water instead of milk you will get Irish moss jelly.

A glass of hot milk with a teaspoonful of soaked Irish moss and some honey dissolved in it is soothing for a child's chest cold.

Dried carragheen can be stored and used exactly the same as the fresh weed—good for thickening soups and stews.

Dulse

A red-coloured seaweed plentiful on the middle and lower shores (Latin, *Rhodymenia palmata*). Use either raw in salads or fry the dried fronds and crumble them to make a savoury relish. It is very tough and if used as a cooked vegetable it needs up to five hours' simmering.

Kelp

Large, brown-coloured seaweeds (*Laminaria*) growing at the low-water mark. The variety *L. digitata* can be used as carragheen above or raw and chopped as a salad ingredient.

Laver

Purple laver (*Porphyra umbilicalis*) and green laver (*Ulva latissima*) are other common seaweeds around our coasts. These are the smooth, line seaweeds which cling to rocks like wet, brown silk. Very popular in parts of Wales, where it is sold in the shops, and in eighteenth-century Bath 'fine potted laver' was a street cry.

To make laver sauce for mutton, boil to a stiff, green mush (do this in a double saucepan as it sticks easily) like spinach. Transfer this to a jar and it will keep for several days. When you are ready to serve it, use two cupfuls and add a walnut-sized piece of butter and the juice of a lemon (or Seville bitter orange). Beat it well.

Sea lettuce

Plentiful at those places where water runs into the sea. This seaweed (*Ulva lactuca*) can be enjoyed as a green vegetable or cooked like laver. Less common, but more delicate, is a seaweed very like sea lettuce called *Monostroma grevillei*.

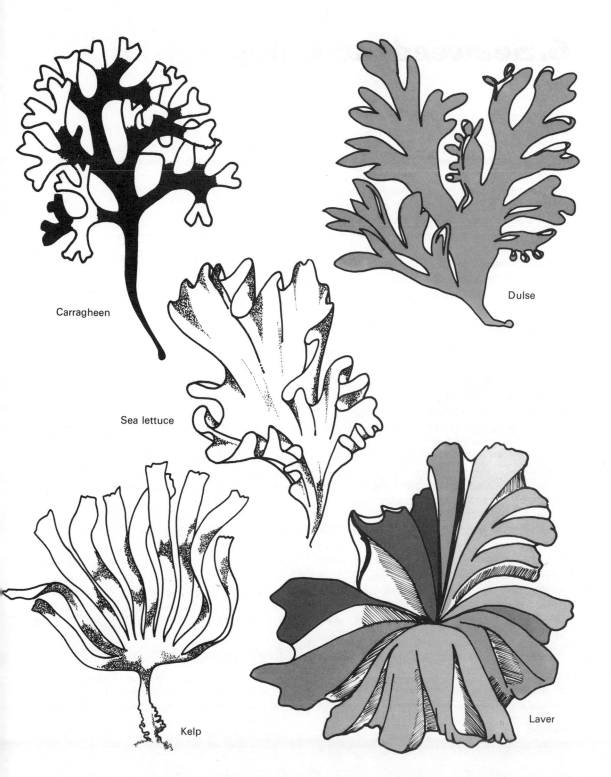

Carragheen

Dulse

Sea lettuce

Kelp

Laver

Flowers Needing Protection

About 1,300 different wild flowering plants grow in the British Isles. When you are in the countryside looking for the edible free plants listed in this book you may come across plants which are now so rare that they are threatened with extinction—so, whether legally protected or not, *please do not pick them*—however attractive the flowers. Here is an alphabetical list of the twenty plants most in danger:

Alpine catchfly (*Lychnis alpina*). Pink flowers, 50–150 mm (2–6 in.), Highlands and Lake District.

Alpine gentian (*Gentiana nivalis*). Blue flowers, 25–150 mm (1–6 in.), on a few Highland mountains.

Alpine sow-thistle (*Cicerbita alpina*). 0.6–1.8 m (2–6 ft.), Highlands.

Cheddar pink (*Dianthus gratianopolitanus*). Pink flowers, 50–230 mm (2–9 in.), Somerset and a few other places.

Diapensia (*Diapensia lapponica*). Cream flowers on an evergreen plant, up to 50 mm (2 in.), Inverness-shire.

Drooping saxifrage (*Saxifraga cernua*). White flowers, 150 mm (6 in.), on Highland mountains.

Fritillary (*Fritillaria meleagris*). Chequered purplish flowers, 200–500 mm (8–20 in.), damp meadows in southern England.

Gladiolus (*Gladiolus illyricus*). Magenta flowers, 0.6 m (2 ft.), New Forest, Hampshire.

Lady's slipper orchid (*Cypripedium calceolus*). Brown and yellow flowers, 300 mm (12 in.), West Yorkshire.

Mezereon (*Daphne mezereum*). Pink flowers, up to 0.9 m (3 ft.), chalky woodlands in England (see also Appendix II, on poisonous plants).

Mountain heath (*Phyllodoce caerulea*). Pink flowers, 200 mm (8 in.), Perthshire.

Military orchid (*Orchis militaris*). Pink flowers, 200–450 mm (8–18 in.), Suffolk and the Chilterns.

Monkey orchid (*Orchis simia*). Pink flowers (rather deeper colour but smaller than the military orchid), 200–500 mm (8–20 in.), Kent and the Chilterns.

Pasque flower (*Pulsatilla vulgaris*). Purple flowers, 50–100 mm (2–4 in.), chalky pastures from Cotswolds to Lincolnshire.

Red helleborine (*Cephalanthera rubra*). Scarlet flowers, 0.3–0.6 m (1–2 ft.), Cotswolds and Buckinghamshire.

Spiked speedwell (*Veronica spicata*). Blue flowers, 100–600 mm (4–24 in.), Norfolk and West Country.

Spring gentian (*Gentiana verna*). Deep blue flowers, 25–100 mm (1–4 in.), Upper Teesdale and Co. Clare in Ireland.

Snowdon lily (*Lloydia serotina*). Pale pink flowers, 50–150 mm (2–6 in.), north and mid-Wales.

Teesdale sandwort (*Minuartia stricta*). White flowers, 75–300 mm (3–12 in.), Upper Teesdale.

Tufted saxifrage (*Saxifraga cespitosa*). Cream flowers, 150 mm (6 in.), mountains in the Highlands.

Poisonous Plants

The following flowering plants, shrubs and trees are, even if not always clinically poisonous, at least dangerous or unwise to eat (poisonous fungi are listed in a separate volume in this series):

Alder buckthorn (Berry-bearing alder)—*Frangula alnus*
Baneberry—*Actaea spicata*
Bittersweet (Woody nightshade)—*Solanum dulcamara*
Black bryony—*Tamus communis*
Black nightshade—*Solanum nigrum*
Buttercup, all species—*Ranunculus*
Columbine—*Aquilegia vulgaris*
Common buckthorn—*Rhamnus catharticus*
Cowbane—*Cicuta virosa*
Darnel rye-grass—*Lolium temulentum*
Deadly nightshade—*Atropa belladonna*
Dog's mercury—*Mercurialis perennis*
Fine-leaved water dropwort—*Oenanthe aquatica*
Fool's parsley—*Aethusa cynapium*
Foxglove—*Digitalis purpurea*
Fritillary—*Fritillaria meleagris*
Green hellebore—*Helleborus viridis*
Hemlock—*Conium maculatum*
Hemlock water dropwort—*Oenanthe crocata*
Henbane—*Hyoscyamus niger*
Ivy—*Hedera helix*
Lily of the valley—*Convallaria majalis*
Meadow saffron—*Colchicum autumnale*
Mezereon—*Daphne mezereum*
Mistletoe—*Viscum album*
Monkshood—*Aconitum anglicum*
Privet—*Ligustrum vulgare*
Spindle-tree—*Euonymus europaeus*
Spurges—*Euphorbiaceae*
Spurge-laurel—*Daphne laureola*
Stinking hellebore—*Helleborus foetidus*
Thorn-apple—*Datura stramonium*
Tubular water dropwort—*Oenanthe fistulosa*
White bryony—*Bryonia dioica*
Yew—*Taxus baccata*

Note: In all cases of suspected poisoning see your doctor immediately, because the action of some plant poisons is rapid.

Nature's Medicines from Seed

Throughout this book many references have been made to the medieval herbalists' and physicians' use of wild plants; also to the proven health-giving properties of certain herbs and to the plant sources of some of today's drugs.

Readers who have a garden may like to have a short list of herbal remedies which, if the plants as listed in this book cannot be found in sufficient quantities in the wild, can be grown from seed obtainable from certain specialist seedsmen in this country. These plants —additional to the more well-known garden herbs—are:

Lemon balm. Used, like tranquillisers, for relaxation of nervous conditions, relieving tooth-ache and reducing high temperature.

Pennyroyal. Herbalists advise its use against depression and for easing an upset stomach. (But women should not take pennyroyal when pregnant.)

Peppermint. Familiar enough as a relief in various kinds of indigestion and sickness. Some herbalists claim it is good for migraine.

Wild parsley. It has a long history as being helpful in cases of anaemia, rheumatism and jaundice. Also used in the treatment of boils.

Yarrow. A herbal tea recommended for relieving colds and influenza. Also useful in cases of diarrhoea.

Preparation of herbal remedies mostly consists of putting the leaves in a teapot and pouring on boiling water to extract their inherent properties, be they protein, vitamins or vital minerals.

Further Reading

The British Flora, Bentham and Hooker (Reeve)
British Flowering Plants, Mederis and Bangerter (Ward Lock)
British Poisonous Plants, A. A. Forsyth (Ministry of Agriculture Bulletin)
English Recipes, Sheila Hutchins (Methuen)
The Englishman's Flora, Geoffrey Grigson (Paladin)
Food in England, Dorothy Hartley (Macdonald)
Gerard's Herball (1636), ed. Marcus Woodward (Spring Books)
Herbal Remedies, Simmonite and Culpeper (Foulsham)
Medicinal Plants, Hans Fluck, translated from German by J. M. Rowson, Professor of
    Pharmacy in the University of Bradford (Foulsham)
The Oxford Book of Wild Flowers, B. E. Nicholson (O.U.P.)
Pick, Cook and Brew, Susan Beedell (Mayflower)
The Survival Handbook, Michael Allaby (Macmillan)
Wild Fruits and Nuts, Geoffrey Eley (EP Publishing, 1976)

Index of Plant Names